If you have longed—re
God better along wit
biblical and practical s
be pursued in multiple areas, then these meditations are for
you. Designed to add layer upon layer of growth in order to
achieve our depth completely in Christ, such wisdom is not
often found. These meditations are recommended for the
pursuit of God.

Gary R. Habermas
Distinguished Research Professor,
Liberty University, Lynchburg, Virginia

One of the most wonderful promises Christ has given us is
to be with us always, but what does it mean to practise His
presence and enjoy His transforming friendship? Here is a
remarkable book of meditations on one of the most vital but
most neglected aspects of Christian living. Every page is rich
in biblical wisdom to be savoured phrase by phrase. If you
read slowly and reflect prayerfully, this sharply focused book
will deepen your devotion to Christ, nurture your inner life,
and align your thoughts with eternity.

Jonathan Lamb
Author, Bible teacher, and minister-at-large,
Keswick Ministries

Deep Simplicity

MEDITATIONS ON
ABIDING IN CHRIST

EMILY DARNELL

CHRISTIAN
FOCUS

10 9 8 7 6 5 4 3 2 1

Copyright © 2020 Emily Darnell

paperback ISBN: 978-1-5271-0589-8
epub ISBN: 978-1-5271-0657-4
mobi ISBN: 978-1-5271-0658-1

Published in 2020
by
Christian Focus Publications,
Geanies House, Fearn, Tain,
Ross-shire, IV20 1TW,
Great Britain

Cover design by Pete Barnsley
Printed and bound by Bell & Bain, Glasgow

Contents

Acknowledgements

I want to express my wholehearted thanks to God for:

My family, and their support along the writing journey. This book could not have come about if it were not for the encouragement of my husband, Russell Darnell, and my children, William and Vivian.

My pastor, Tre Smith, who encourages me to grow in grace and knowledge, and to use my gifts in the church.

My friends who have prayed for me along the way. Especially the ladies in my church, who have shared life with me over the years.

And thank you, Christian Focus, for working with me, it has been a delight. Thank you Sandra Byatt for your work editing this book, and your encouragement to me as a writer.

1

Introduction

We are called to abide. Have you ever wondered what that entails? The journey of faith each of us is on was begun, and will continue, by the Spirit. As we sojourn here on earth, He will by His gentleness and patience draw us ever closer, grace upon grace. Deep will call unto deep, as the Lord's deep grace and mercy answer our deep longings and needs. The depth of His love will drown our deeply felt loneliness, the depth of His mercy will not be fathomed by the depth of our depravity, and His deep power and goodness will more than suffice as we face our deep cowardice and lack of virtue. His deep love and grace overcome our deep misery. He holds us, keeps us from stumbling, transforms us, and will one day bring us safely home. Meanwhile we sojourn here, and as we do we are called to abide in Him. The life He calls us to is one of abiding ever deeper in Him. Abiding is simple, though it doesn't always seem easy.

There is nothing new under the sun, so naturally the readers of this book have already pondered, and perhaps read other books about abiding in Christ. Maybe John 15 is even one of your favorite chapters, or 1 John one of your favorite Epistles. Without a doubt, this is a topic which will be encouraging to all believers until Christ takes us home. It is good to be reminded of these truths, and it is particularly edifying to remain in these doctrines for the grace and strength we gain therein.

The meditations presented in this book are the fruit of many seasons in my personal walk with the Lord. There were far too many moments of having not tasted or seen God's goodness, many days of not believing God's presence in my life. In conversations with a dear friend, we referred to these as 'dark days.' Over many cups of coffee, we prayed and encouraged one another through seasons of dark days. Over the years I've learned that my feelings in those moments were trumping Jesus as the way, the truth and the life. He calls out 'seek My face' and I respond 'I don't want to – I want You to seek me and remove me from all unpleasant situations.' He would remind me of His firm grip and His everlasting arms, and I would say 'but …' endlessly, always coming up with a reason for doubting His goodness towards me. In abiding, I have learned to overcome these overwhelming feelings, laying them at the foot of the cross. By abiding in, or remaining in, God's Word I have found the grace to walk through dark seasons. By abiding in God's love, I have learned to silence the doubts that creep into my thoughts. In fellowship with others I have experienced the joy of sharing this grace and His Word, a means of grace so often missed in this world. Jesus promised tribulations for all of His followers in this world, and in the midst of those tribulations He also promises to be our joy and peace. Those days wherein you have no taste for God's Word are the days you need to abide in it most. To abide is to remain, to rest, to dwell, to be at home. Abiding is active, mutual, soul-satisfying, all-encompassing.

Devotion to Christ

Devotion to Christ is quite often mistaken for what this generation calls 'devotions,' a quick snippet of time with the Lord and I'm set for the day. Read a book that references a verse and walk away to get on with real life. Well as you may have guessed, this is not one of those sorts of books, rather it is written with the desire that readers will run back to Scripture, dig deeper, cling to it, write it on your own hearts, and think upon it throughout every day of your sojourning. At the heart of what Jesus taught in His call to abide is that abiding is not a task, nor a moment, rather it is living life in His presence. In all moments, to do all things with Him and for Him and through Him (see Rom. 11:36, perhaps meditate on it). This call to abide is for all believers, it is for you beloved.

People are easily deceived. All people, regardless of social standing or education or upbringing or current church membership status, can be deceived easily. Even believers who are set upon the truth and have found that the truth really does set us free, are not yet in a place where they cannot be deceived. Paul worried for the Colossians that someone would come along with plausible or 'persuasive arguments' and draw them away (see Col. 2:4). Jesus told His disciples that false teachers would deceive even the elect if He had not set a limit (see Matt. 24:24).

This same idea is emphasized in Paul's second letter to the Corinthians, wherein he warns that even those who are seeking truth can be very easily led astray from it. It is quite possible that our 'minds will be led astray from the simplicity and purity of devotion to Christ' (see 2 Cor. 11:3). Led astray from what, and how can this be? Led away from simplicity, when we complicate things or add to what Christ has revealed. We tend to excuse Christians who do this when we believe they really love God. Love will lead them back to the simplicity and purity, and would not let them continue in their own version of pleasing Christ. We are also in danger of being led astray from purity when we are devoted to 'Christ and,' rather than Christ alone. Or when we are double-minded (see James 1:8 and 4:8) concerning our belief in God's goodness and power. Or when we are more devoted to an agenda for our lives that is not first and foremost concerned about God's glory. When our desires are not in line with God's, we will soon discover ourselves to be walking on the broad path, rather than His narrow one.

Devoted in Heart, Soul, Mind, and Body

Christ, who is the Word made flesh, does not change, therefore devotion to Him transcends cultural changes. Devotion does not change with the passing of time. It is Scripture that will encourage and build us up, rather than new or different forms of what some would call worship. Devotion to Christ must be understood as an active state of being that has bearing on our mental, emotional, and physical self. He has revealed Himself in simplicity; there is one Lord, one Word, one Body. Yet we try to serve several lords, or we insist there can be many bodies with many opposing teachings (viewpoints, some may say). One Spirit is at work uniting us in His love, granting His true church perseverance, endurance, fortitude. He will draw His true church deeper and deeper into the true knowledge of Himself, speaking a deeper wisdom to us as we mature (see 1 Cor. 2). The Spirit also draws us deeper into the renewal our souls long for and into the true knowledge of who we really are. The Spirit draws us deeper into His manifold wisdom, and of the glorious plans He has for us. It is not 'flesh and blood' that will reveal any of this to us, it is the

'Father who is in heaven' who wills it to be known, and who sends His Spirit of truth to illumine our understanding (Matt. 16:17).

To understand the role of the Spirit in illumining our minds, there are many passages to study; spend some time in John 14–17, 1 Corinthians 2, and 1 John. There is no program for us to engage in, this is His work alone. We come to the Word, and the Spirit grants understanding as a light shining in the dark revealing what is truly there. He continues this work by growing us into an understanding of His deep wisdom, of His thoughts which are higher than ours, a wisdom which can only be understood by those united to Christ, as God was pleased to hide all this wisdom in Christ. We see only dimly, but the Spirit will enable you to see that delightful vision. Paul instructed Timothy to study Scripture without engaging with the useless words of others (see 2 Tim. 2:14-18). This should be the way for all disciples of Jesus. We cannot mishandle His Word, ignore it, add modern viewpoints to it, or think studying it is for elders alone.

'Manifest' is another of those words used often in Scripture that ought to be defined. To make manifest is to put on display, to make it known by leading it out to be seen. Jesus says if we have seen Him, we have seen the Father, because He came as the image of the invisible, making God manifest. When Jesus turned water to wine, we are told that: 'This beginning of His signs Jesus did in Cana of Galilee, and manifested His glory, and His disciples believed in Him' (John 2:11). Jesus made God manifest, He led God out to be seen, to be known. We can know, and we can grow in this knowledge, as we abide in Him.

As reasonable creatures we need to daily, prayerfully, and actively engage our minds in His Word, which He uses to renew all facets of our being. Devotion to Christ is daily. Moment by moment, in all our quotidian affairs, in the midst of (and indeed sanctifying) our vocations. One's devotion to Christ is manifest in the fruit we bear in all our relations and endeavors.

Devotion to Christ is akin to abiding. To abide is to rest, to dwell, but it is not to sit idly by. It is to lean into Jesus' bosom and listen to His words of eternal life. It is to taste those words, muse upon them, and orient our lives around them. Continually. To understand His words is to obey them, for in understanding we grasp it with our whole being and it is manifest inseparably in both our words and deeds.

The call to abide, and to be devoted, is also a call to prepare your minds for action (1 Pet. 1:13). As you read this book, have your Bible at hand, and read the Scripture references. As you do so, know that you are an active party in this most wonderful relationship. We seek, He seeks. We cling, and He holds us. We hope, and discover that God has given us assurance. We are renewed as we wait on Him who renews. We are always becoming our true selves as He conforms us to the image of Christ. We are a partaker in His suffering and glory, rather than any substitute glory, knowing all the while that as we abide in God so He abides in us. Each chapter will unfold an aspect of abiding, ending with some practices to incorporate in personal worship, or Scriptures to meditate upon to grow deeper in grace, and in knowledge and love of the one who loved you first.

2

Seeking

We seek because we are created for fellowship with God. We crave that fellowship, that mutual abiding, that dwelling together inseparably. We long for it, and we will always be seeking after something to satisfy that longing. God rewards those who seek Him, He is indeed good to those who seek Him (Heb. 11:6; Lam. 3:25). He does not reward merely with the passing goods of this world, but with a reward that satisfies our deepest soul longings, and that brings Him the most glory while drawing us further into His glory. His eternal plans for us are good, including both a hope and a future. But that hope is not fulfilled here in the land corrupted by the fall; that future has nothing to do with our idolatrous materialistic dreams. Will we be those who seek Him, and worship Him, in spirit and in truth? Or among those who seek something lesser (less rewarding even), and strive to find merely a kernel of truth that remains in His creation without coming to Him? Are we crying out after earthly goods, merely physical relief, and a life without mishap? Or do we cry out for Him, longing for God to make all things new and to fulfill all He has promised? Have you pondered what God has promised to His children?

Read this, and then let your heart pray with the Psalmist:

> *When You said,* 'Seek My face,' my heart said to You,
> 'Your face, O LORD, I shall seek' (Ps. 27:8).

> [I shall] Seek the LORD and His strength;
> Seek His face continually.
> [I shall] Remember His wonders which He has done, …'
> (Ps. 105:4-5).

We seek with our whole being, and He discloses Himself. As promised, He does not remain hidden, but delights to open our eyes that we may see Him and know Him. He will ever remain true to His promise of letting us find Him, and find our life in Him, and of growing us deeper in that all-encompassing knowledge. He tells believers to open the door for He is standing there, knocking. This is not an invitation to salvation. This is a call to return to Jesus (who is your first love), to open the door to Him, to seek Him where He is to be found (see Rev. 2:4, 3:20). When we seek, we find that He's taken the initiative all along! He speaks. He woos. He draws us with His everlasting love. Thus we seek and realize we have never been alone. We pray and become attentive toward His words – we pray in the Spirit by engaging with the 'sword of the Spirit' (see Eph. 6:17). We seek truly by turning prayerfully to His Word; letting His Word guide our hearts as we pray. This is not groping about in the darkness, for He is the light that shines in our hearts, that enlightens us (see 2 Cor. 4:6-7). And so we seek despite emotions and doubts and souls filled with angst telling us otherwise.

We do so easily go astray, as we set idols before us and follow them with all our hearts. Nevertheless, He is a faithful husbandman tending His vineyard (remember John 15). Here in this world the true children of God will experience

His pruning. Good things that keep us back from seeing and enjoying Him, from seeking Him, and from finding our identity in Him are cut away from us. Our heart's cry in one of these moments will reveal to us our own dependency that was misplaced in the passing things of this world, in the shifting shadows of idols. He circumcised our hearts once, and He will ever faithfully chasten us until we are safely home.

Ponder for a moment, the connection between the promises of God, the accomplishments of Christ, and what they secure for us:

> … and in Him you were also circumcised with a circumcision made without hands in the removal of the body of the flesh by the circumcision of Christ; having been buried with Him in baptism, in which you were also raised up with Him through faith in the working of God, who raised Him from the dead. When you were dead in your transgressions and the uncircumcision of your flesh, He made you alive together with Him, having forgiven us all our transgressions (Col. 2:11-13).

> Moreover the LORD your God will circumcise your heart and the heart of your descendants, to love the LORD your God with all your heart and with all your soul, so that you may live (Deut. 30:6).

> And I will give them one heart, and put a new spirit within them. And I will take the heart of stone out of their flesh and give them a heart of flesh, that they may walk in My statutes and keep My ordinances and do them. Then they will be My people, and I shall be their God(Ezek. 11:19-20).

Abiding in Christ, we find our security in His promises and in His works on our behalf. We rest in the knowledge that He has circumcised our hearts, and made us alive, that we may be His people.

Meditate

We seek Him by looking to Him as He has revealed Himself; Christ crucified, resurrected, and ascended into heaven where He ever lives to intercede on our behalf. We seek by coming to Him who alone has words of eternal life (see John 6:59-71) and in whom are hidden all the treasures of wisdom and knowledge (Col. 2:1-3). We participate in this great work of His by meditating on His Word, which takes intentional time. Setting aside time for this regularly will enable you the rest of your day to briefly turn your thoughts towards His truth and beauty and goodness whether working, driving, performing quotidian tasks or fretting over what to do next.

We meditate as we focus on His Word while silencing all the contrary voices of this world. Sometimes, this means spending a moment listing out all the 'to do' items that choke out this time; write them down and save them for later. Then focus on a portion of Scripture knowing you can get to those other things in due time. Give yourself at least ten minutes to read, re-read, copy, and muse upon the passage. The truth has set you free, you are free to fight the contrary thoughts, focus on truth and let the truth wash over you and fill you. Meditate on the thought for a moment that you really were raised with Christ, that He did not merely clean up your heart but gave you a new one. The beauty of Christian meditation is that we do not empty our minds in search of inner anything. Rather we come to the God of the universe who promises to meet us, fill us, teach us, reveal Himself to us, and renew us to a true knowledge.

Your new heart is capable of meditating on, understanding, and loving eternal things. Capable also of experiencing the joy and peace God longs to give, and of believing that His glory is worth your attention and striving. The Word of the

Lord is faithful and enduring; we can trust these promises. As we meditate, let us turn these promises from Colossians and Deuteronomy and Ezekiel into prayers, and thereby strengthen our hearts that would otherwise grow weary. This is the very exercise of abiding in His words that Jesus asked His disciples to engage in, and we would do well to grow in this habit. Abide in His Word, let His words direct your heart, and your affections will change, and as they do your prayers will change.

We seek, and we find that He all along was seeking us, setting His affections upon us. We seek by purifying our hearts of all the lies that ensnare, and of the voices of lesser lovers that call us away from our true selves and our true lover. Set them aside, do not let them be the lens through which you read Scripture. Sometimes we need to honestly ask ourselves: do we want the depth God offers? The treasures He offers? Or do we want merely to feel good in our own earthly pursuits? Do we long for His glory, which He so eagerly came to call us into (John 17; 2 Thess. 2:13-15) or do we satisfy our hearts with glory from one another (John 5:44)? As you intentionally meditate on Scriptures speaking to these struggles, He will continue to prune. The Lord will mercifully show you your heart's contrary desires that you may crucify them. He will do this so that you can seek Him more deeply with your whole heart, He will not be satisfied to share your heart with lesser loves.

As we are to love the Lord our God with all our heart, soul, mind and strength, so we are to seek Him with our whole being. Any one of these aspects may at times control the others, drawing us away from the simplicity and purity of devotion, of abiding. We feel emotionally parched in a desert. We grow tired and weary. We lose sight of true logic and reasoning. We are easily distracted and our seeking lasts but a moment. Stand firm beloved! Let your heart take courage and comfort! Fight the good fight of the faith, the faith that was once for all handed down to us (see Jude). It is not that we cannot read Scripture for more than five minutes, it is that we have trained our brains to be captivated by every little thought that enters in, and grow weary by pondering, meditating, finding connections, studying, and delighting in the Word. We sometimes accept worldly labels that make us believe we cannot abide or rest, we cannot sit at His feet and learn because we must go accomplish a task. This makes seeking the grace we need (for our heart, soul, mind and body) at the foot of the cross difficult, but not impossible. We can train our brains in the ways of the world, or in the patterns God reveals. The world offers us a false sense of self sufficiency, angst, and relational friction as we use others rather than love others. The Word invites us instead to put off that old self, put on the new (see Eph. 4:17-24), and to put others' needs ahead of ours as we love them more than our own momentary comfort. Our old habits can be broken by the Spirit who dwells in us. New habits can be formed, habits of grace. We do not look to the law to change us, rather we are led by the Spirit (see Gal. 5). And after a season of putting on these habits daily, or seasonally, your whole being will enjoy a renewal that allows you to delight in them. In this renewal, you will not so easily be persuaded to cease abiding in Christ (see Col. 2:6–3:11).

Pure Milk

Putting on the new, and beginning these habits of grace will start small and grow. Be patient with yourself as you begin, as you continue. Peter has the most beautiful illustration when he tells the believers in various churches scattered abroad that they ought to at first crave for and drink the pure milk of

God's Word as a baby nurses from his mother. This imagery is fascinating to a new parent, who cannot sleep more than three hours at a time because of the new baby's need for milk. The cry for milk awakens any mother, and the baby happily sucks all that is available before drifting back off to sleep, or perhaps enjoying a few moments of contented wakefulness. This immature season in our spiritual lives can be exciting, but there are some who do not enter in, or strive to grow through it. They are overwhelmed by all they do not know, and instead of crying out for milk and happily drinking it in, they become mere attenders of church and forsake really fellowshipping. They deny the power of God's Word by letting it collect dust. Peter and Paul, inspired by the Spirit, have harsh words for such behavior.

There can be no abiding in Christ apart from the Word. There is no seeking after God if we forsake that which He has revealed. Do not be overwhelmed at the amount of knowledge or the enormity of the call. The important thing to remember is simply to set time aside. He is gentle and will gently lead you. Morning and evening, open and close your day with the Alpha and Omega, the Beginning and the End. Reading a portion in these times will prepare you for meditating on His Word as David did, as God calls us all to (read Psalm 1). Slowly add in more time, different times, and different weekly habits. Daily make time to read, pray, muse upon, sing, and delight in the Lord. Read from both testaments, seeing how they both point us to Christ and reveal God's plan of redemption which spans from before creation through the founding of His church. God's character is revealed in beautiful ways in some of the Old Testament books that believers shy away from reading. Set weekly times for more in-depth study, writing in a journal, meditation and memorization, corporate singing, hearing the Word preached, fellowship and serving. Create spontaneous times for extra reading, journaling, fellowship or corporate worship, as you are led by the Spirit.

Prior to having children, I would awaken to an alarm clock, pray, then get up for a morning routine which included Bible reading and coffee, shower, breakfast, and leaving for work. As a mother I awaken a bit more tired than I used to, so I found new ways to set my mind on the Spirit. I have the words from a favorite hymn in a very artistic manner framed near to both the coffee pot and window in my kitchen. I stumble in to start cooking breakfast and pack lunches, and see, 'Awake my Soul and Sing!' to which my heart delights, I sing, I pray and the quotidian tasks are transformed into a time of worship and service, of partaking in something grand. Find something that helps draw your attention to your glorious God, that your first waking moments may be with Him, rather than in dread of another day, or in prideful planning, or otherwise occupied in mindlessly moving along. Routines change in various seasons of life, but making time to dwell on the Word must always be a priority.

We cannot grow lazy or give in to self pity, which are some of the quickest and most cunning enemies of our seeking and abiding. To continually seek Him, to seek to know Him more deeply, is part of the obedience of faith to which we are called (see Rom. 1:5 and 16:26 to see a link between faith and obedience). Do not lose heart, do not simply wait for each day to pass and give way to the next. He has died on the cross for us who were once His enemies, the people whom He created for Himself, whom He called and has drawn with His everlasting love (Jer. 31:3), and whom He has created anew in Christ for such works as this (Eph. 2:1-10). As we resolve to seek the one true God, we stand in His grace and He fills us with all the love, joy, and peace we desire (Rom.

5:1-5; 15:13). In these finite bodies and minds, we can only handle a foretaste of what He will reveal in heaven. But that taste is sweet, and worth every moment of seeking.

Be still, listen to His Word, and you will hear what you are seeking for. Thus you will hear of the love that sanctifies and will not let you go, and of your belonging. Belonging to God, and to the community He has created. 'Everyone who is of the truth hears My voice' (John 18:37). Do not be like the scores of idolaters who try to listen apart from His Word. He has made Himself manifest, He has promised to disclose Himself, but He does not do so apart from His appointed means, His Word. Jesus answered this question directly toward the end of His ministry, about how and to whom He would reveal Himself, in John 14:21-24:

> He who has My commandments and keeps them is the one who loves Me; and he who loves Me will be loved by My Father, and I will love him and will disclose Myself to him. Judas (not Iscariot) said to Him, 'Lord, what then has happened that You are going to disclose Yourself to us and not to the world?' Jesus answered and said to him, 'If anyone loves Me, he will keep My word; and My Father will love him, and We will come to him and make Our abode with him. He who does not love Me does not keep My words; and the word which you hear is not Mine but the Father's who sent Me.'

Open your Bible and read expectantly. The Spirit reveals the depths of God to us, teaching us true spiritual thoughts, 'that we may know the things freely given to us by God' (see 1 Cor. 2:12). If you read and your heart is rarely enlarged, your emotions unaffected, your thoughts not re-aligned, then you may need to approach the text differently. Are you coming to Scripture as to any other book, trying to interpret and apply as you see fit? Or do you come believing this is His Word, and the interpretation belongs to Him, and He will teach you, disclosing Himself to you? Do you come humbly desiring to be taught, or do you come feeling you are educated enough to read it all and understand at will? Do you come prayerfully, dependent on Him for light and life? Do you come as a little child wanting to listen to his Father, trusting that He knows everything?

Practices

Hermeneutics is the science and art of understanding a text. It is important to read all books, but especially Scripture, within context, within genre, looking for the author's intended meaning rather than superimposing our own. As you approach your times of reading and studying, do not ask 'what does this mean to me?' or 'how does this make me feel?' Scripture is not designed to be used to feed our egos, the interpretation is not ours to finagle. Here are a few healthy questions to ask about each text you approach:

- Who was the original audience? What was happening in their history at the time this was being given? What was their culture like? Where geographically were they, and how does that impact the meaning?
- How does this section point me to Christ?
- What genre of literature is this? How does that affect my understanding of word choice, imagery, or literary devices?
- What does the word choice tell me about how to understand this passage? Are there active or passive verbs? Are these singular or plural nouns? Is this past tense, ongoing, or future?
- How does this passage line up with all of Scripture, all of redemptive history?

Seek out a Bible Encyclopedia, a Bible Atlas, and some good commentaries to help answer the first set of questions mentioned above. In addition to your own pastor, it is helpful to have teachers and theologians in your life. My favorite teachers/theologians to read are John Owen (I would start with *The Glory of Christ*) and Jonathan Edwards (I would start with *Charity and Its Fruits*), or John Stott (try *The Cross of Christ*).

Set aside time for further study on the concept of seeking God: Amos 5:4, 6,14; Zephaniah 2:3; 1 Chronicles 22:18-19; 28:9; Joel 2:12-13; John 5:37-47; John 6:66-69; Romans 2:7-11, 6:16-22; Colossians 3; 1 Peter 2:9-10. Find the connections between these passages and rejoice that God has been revealing Himself to us!

Redeem the time that would normally be 'down time,' wasted time. Rather than the 'usual' which for most in this generation is social media, read some verses detailing God's promises to lead you, to sustain you, to keep you, to lavish grace upon you. Ponder how when you are weary of seeking, you are being held. We do not seek because He has gone away from us, we seek and realize He is abiding with us still. This will aid in turning our self pity and introspection into gazing at the God of all beauty, all truth, all grace and mercy, purpose, strength, and comfort. We continually abide when we fight for these times, rather than tossing them into the wind. After fighting for them a bit, they become an ingrained part of us. We abide in His Word when we treasure our times learning and meditating more than our times of merely 'shutting off our brains' for meaningless breaks.

Commit Psalm 1:1-3 to memory, and as you meditate on the imagery used, find other passages using similar metaphors. Journal these together and delight in the large picture the Lord may be showing you.

3

Clinging

A s we grow in abiding, seeking leads to clinging. Take
some time to read Deuteronomy 32:1-12. Herein God's
people are called to hear, to remember, and to consider. We
are told that this teaching distills, refreshes, renews. Listen to
this passage, let it soak in as the spring rains refresh the earth.
God created us for this relationship (see Ps. 139; Isa. 43:7;
Eph. 1 and 2). When the triune God created the world,
God the Son especially rejoiced to see the plan unfold (see
Prov. 8, keeping in mind that Jesus is wisdom personified).
The relationship between God and His people glorifies and
delights Him. God created for His own glory and calls us
into this glory.

When God first called Israel to Himself and gave the
command to 'cling' it was new, groundbreaking. Other
countries with their false religions did not cling to a god,
gods were to be appeased, not trusted as they were fickle.
The one true God can be both trusted and clung to. He does
not change, He does not forsake, His power and justice are
unmatched. So are His love and mercy. When we cling, we
realize we are in the grasp of the everlasting arms of eternal
love. We realize that we are the apple of God's eye and His

delight. We begin to see what it is to be created in God's image, with a mind, emotions, and will which are capable of knowing Him when released from the power and corruption of sin. As we read the record of redemptive history, we see that God has never diverted from this. Our victor has released us from that corruption, and as we cling we experience that promised work of distilling and refreshing.

Let these passages soak in, as you ponder what it is to cling to God:

> Yet on your fathers did the LORD set His affection to love them, and He chose their descendants after them …You shall fear the LORD your God; you shall serve Him and cling to Him, and you shall swear by His name (Deut 10:15, 20).

> You shall therefore impress these words of mine on your heart and on your soul; and you shall bind them as a sign on your hand, and they shall be as frontals on your forehead. You shall teach them to your sons, talking of them when you sit in your house and when you walk along the road and when you lie down and when you rise up. For if you are careful to keep all this commandment which I am commanding you to do, to love the LORD your God, to walk in all His ways and hold fast to Him (Deut. 11:18-19, 22).

> You shall follow the LORD your God and fear Him; and you shall keep His commandments, listen to His voice, serve Him, and cling to Him (Deut. 13:4).

> For you are a holy people to the LORD your God and the LORD has chosen you to be a people for His own possession out of all the peoples who are on the face of the earth(Deut. 14:2).

> The LORD has today declared you to be His people, a treasured possession, as He promised you, and that you should keep all His commandments; and that He will set you high above all

nations which He has made, for praise, fame, and honor; and that you shall be a consecrated people to the LORD your God, as He has spoken (Deut. 26:18-19).

So choose life in order that you may live, you and your descendants, by loving the LORD your God, by obeying His voice, and by holding fast to Him; for this is your life and the length of your days … (Deut. 30:19b-20a).

The LORD is the one who goes ahead of you; He will be with you. He will not fail you or forsake you. Do not fear or be dismayed (Deut. 31:8).

The exhortation to cling to the Lord is never separated from interacting with His Word. We cling to the God who reveals Himself, we know God because of His revealing Word. We listen to His voice therein, we believe, we remember, we obey, and we cling to Him. From this posture we serve because as we find our life source from God, as the branch does from the vine, it flows out in service. We serve with our whole being because people cannot be compartmentalized. Cling with heart and soul and mind, then serve in prayer and word and deed.

Word of Life, Word of Power

Much like the original call to cling, the New Testament church is told to cling, or hold fast to, the Word of life (Phil. 2:12-16). The fruit of this clinging, of letting God's Word abide in us, cannot be produced by flesh, by any sort of self-effort. And like any other fruit it does not ripen immediately. The vine provides all the nutrients and is the source of life for all the branches. Likewise, in clinging to the vine, the branches bear fruit. The branches do not do any of the work, but in living connected and abiding lives they glorify the vine. Like all the deep works of God, the fruit of clinging, of abiding, mysteriously grows. As we cling to the Word of life, we come to 'adorn the doctrine of God' (see Titus 2:10) and both our inner and outer life reflect God's Word rather than reflecting the passing and ever shifting words of this world.

As we cling, abiding in God's Word, our true self shines in His light, and comes to the surface. We look away from the flesh and our own self effort and set our thoughts and affections on the Spirit, and on the sword of the Spirit which is the Word of God. Then we cling to 'the word of His power' (see Heb. 1:3) and gain the victory of faith, for He is more powerful than any other of the gods in this world. His Word will silence the other voices we've clung to, the lies we've believed and the plausible arguments that have fooled us. His Word will be powerful in our life when we look to it as the Thessalonians did, believing it to be powerful, and when we look at it as the Psalmist who claimed it to be better than all the riches we could desire.

We cling to God and the power of His resurrection (Phil. 2). We cling to God's Word so that our hearts may be strengthened by His grace, rather than clinging merely to physical sources of strength (Heb. 13:9). We cling, digging our heels into the Word, and happily realize that this is the only way we can stand firm. In Christ, we are not stuck in the moment, nor trapped by self-focus, nor are we left to the devices of our own deceitful hearts. Rather we pour out our hearts before Him, and we listen. His Word is more important, His Word is final. The God who is compassionate, merciful, and abounding in steadfast love will hear, and will disclose Himself. God delights to give us understanding. As we abide in His Word, listening and clinging, His Word will be balm to the heart, and food for the mind and soul.

Clinging is not mere memorization. The Pharisees knew the Scriptures well, Satan had that down too. God's enemies can memorize and use God's words for their purposes. As we cling we will memorize, we will internalize, and impress His words on our hearts. We memorize prayerfully, think upon, and delight in the beauty and meaning that God conveys. We never separate a verse from its true meaning found in relation to the rest of Scripture. Even after we internalize a passage, we still come to God for understanding, for life (remember John 5:39-40). We never become owners of those words, they are God's words eternally. Their meaning comes from Him, the interpretation is His, and the Spirit grants us knowledge and understanding as we come to Him. After we have memorized, how easily we can turn our thoughts into meditations on God's precious words wherever we are.

Israel's great sin, repeated quite often, was forgetting who God was, what He had done and what He had promised or required. In Ezekiel 23:35 for example we read,

> Therefore, thus says the Lord GOD, 'Because you have forgotten Me and cast Me behind your back, bear now the *punishment* of your lewdness and your harlotries.'

In clinging to God's Word, we fight this tendency, and we overcome. We will either train our minds to enjoy endless distractions, and so become enslaved to a short attention span and soundbyte theology; or we will rely on the Spirit's fruit of self-control to help us in memorizing, remembering, recalling, and abiding in His Word. Our flesh has trained our minds in so many contrary ways. But we can crucify those ways, and put them off as we put on and adorn the doctrines of God (see Titus 2:10 and Romans 13:14). We can train our minds in this new way by setting our minds to remember, to remain in His Word.

Cling to the Source

God, the creator of everything, was not created. He has always been, and ever will be. No beginning and no end. He is the Alpha and the Omega. He created space, time, and matter without being bound by anything He created. He has put some bounds upon Himself each time He has made a promise, but no created thing can place a bound upon Him. He alone can do what we refer to as supernatural. He alone has life in Himself, as Jesus taught in John 5:26, 'For just as the Father has life in Himself, even so He gave to the Son also to have life in Himself.' Jesus made sure His disciples heard it plain and clear, 'I am the way, the truth, and the life' (John 14:6). He is the life, we come to Him and to no other for that life we long for. Humankind has always craved getting out of the miseries and bounds of this life-experience, longing for pure beauty and perfection. Jesus speaks to these longings, with His prayer in John 17:2, '…that to all whom You have given Him, He may give eternal life.' The eternal life God gives begins now but will not be fully experienced in this world. Paul reminds Timothy to take hold of the eternal life to which he's been called (1 Tim. 6:12). We must take hold of it, believe His words of life and let them fill your soul and give vitality to your mind and body. Cling to the life, to Jesus, our crucified and risen Lord who gives us life in Himself. Part of our clinging to our source of life, to the eternal life we've been called to, is being willing to re-read Scripture, to memorize, to prayerfully engage in Scripture knowing the Spirit will be enlarging our hearts and minds to take hold of more and more of His life.

> As the living Father sent Me, and I live because of the Father, so he who eats Me, he also will live because of Me … he who eats this bread will live forever (John 6:57-58).

At the most basic level, we need to remember that physical life is not all there is, the physical realm that we currently see, touch, smell and taste is not ultimate. Our daily bread sustains us for a brief moment, but the bread of life sustains our entire being for all the rest of eternity. Our daily earthly bread will typically give us energy for a moment, the bread of life satisfies at a much deeper level, propelling us on to really live with what is ultimate in mind. Eating this bread of life is both a one-time event (salvation) and then an ongoing matter (enjoying life from the source of life) of devotion to Christ, and finding life only in Christ, clinging only to Him. God alone is self-sufficient, that is to say He is the only being with life in Himself. All other life is created by Him, sustained by Him. The Father gave the privilege to His Son to have life in Himself, and we will share in that eternal life only by coming to Jesus who is the way, the truth and the life. Not a moment will pass that we do not need Him, that He is not sustaining us, that we are outside the realm of His sovereign care. And when we consciously choose to be mindful in the moment, to be devoted, to set our minds as He instructs, then we find the life we've been searching for. We find joy and peace in the midst of trials and earthly frustration and sadness. We have sorrow in this world yet are also rejoicing in what is ultimate, eternal, unchanging.

Union With Christ

This particular doctrine, union with Christ, deserves our attention often. To meditate on passages teaching on this union will encourage, fortify, and delight our souls. We are not alone, we are beloved, we belong. And in Christ we are alive, righteous, blameless, fruitful, and heading home. Apart from Him we receive the fruit of our own works: death and separation from God. In union with Him, we receive the reward of eternal life! The quality of which cannot be grasped here and now, though we enjoy the beginnings of it.

Union with Christ promises freedom from the powers that once held us captive: fear, sin, lies, desire for approval. Romans 6 is the most wonderful passage to meditate on slowly, though much of Romans has this 'union' woven through it.

Learning what it means that our old self was crucified with Christ, and our new self is alive in Christ, begs that we focus often throughout our lives on Jesus' death, resurrection, and ascension. Apart from Him we were alienated, hostile enemies of God, choosing evil deeds, though we would excuse them as not so bad really. Read through Colossians 1:13-23 for a riveting account of all this. The focus in Scripture's descriptions of this great work is on what Christ has done for us, is doing for us and in us, and His continual presence in our lives. Union with Christ releases us from all pressure! He will present us holy and blameless! He has rescued us, called us into His kingdom and glory, given us life in Himself and has promised to finish His work, bringing us home to heaven. Because He began this work in us while we were sinners, what great assurance we have that He will continue it. He will be steadfast and make us steadfast as well (see Rom. 5:10; and 8:32).

A Time to Remember

We will cling all the more as we set aside time to remember God's providence throughout all history, the greatness of His salvation, the glory of the cross, the beauty of His infinite plans. Look back at your own chains and ponder the human condition apart from Christ, which was all of us prior to His working in our heart (see Jer. 17:1). Then ponder His solution, His calling, His great love demonstrated at the cross, and His great power demonstrated in the resurrection. Each of us can say with Paul that Jesus 'loved me and gave Himself up for me' (Gal. 2:20).

> ... I have loved you with an everlasting love;
> Therefore I have drawn you with lovingkindness' (Jer. 31:3).

> ... God demonstrates His own love toward us, in that while we were yet sinners, Christ died for us (Rom. 5:8).

We grow weary when we forget God's deeply personal love, His creative and redemptive works, and the wonder of His drawing us into relationship with Him. We abound and flourish in the abundant life when we are mindful. We are to be thoughtfully engaged, clinging as a branch to the vine, drinking deeply the sap full of life, His words of eternal life. Apart from Christ we can know and do nothing. But clinging to the vine, abiding in Him, we as branches are fruitful and experience abundant life, that foretaste of heaven that will fill us with His peace and joy.

Practices

Use the spiritual discipline of journaling to remember. Write out your prayers, the Scriptures you pray through, the verses you need to 'write on the tablet of your heart' (see Prov. 3:3). Copy portions of the catechism or the Westminster Confession with corresponding verses. Write your questions as you read through books of the Bible. When we write, our brains learn the text in ways that we cannot from just reading. We slow down, and muse on the words more carefully when we write them out. When we journal, writing about the text in our own words, our brains learn the text by becoming even more intimate with it. The Psalmist directed his heart to 'muse' upon the Word and works of God and this will help you to as well. Let your heart and mind muse, that you may know Him deeper.

Spend some time asking 'do I manifest the truth?' as Paul spoke of in 2 Corinthians 4:2. What knee-jerk reactions of mine are contrary to God's love and mercy? What fruits can I be studying, praying about, and looking for the Spirit to work in me? What Scripture can I cling to in this process?

Journal through Romans 6:13: 'and do not go on presenting the members of your body to sin as instruments of unrighteousness; but present yourselves to God as those alive from the dead, and your members as instruments of righteousness to God.' Imagine yourself at God's throne, presenting yourself. Imagine His smile, as He calls you beloved and fills you up for today's adventures. Recount what He did to give you that life, you who are alive from the dead. Remember the kingdom of darkness that you were rescued from, and then the kingdom of His beloved Son, and how you became a child of God when He placed you in the latter kingdom.

Psalm 103:2 tells us to 'forget none of His benefits.' Dedicate some time each day, for at least 30 days, to begin the habit of remembering. This is one of those 'seasonal' helps, that perhaps you don't want to think about as a task. Write down all His benefits from the day. He works all things together for His glory and you will see this more clearly if you can look back without forgetting. Be thankful in all things, as you ponder His daily bread and work in your life. Journaling these benefits will encourage your soul in ways that would be missed otherwise, it is good to remember His works, rather than simply acknowledging them at the time. This is why Israel was instructed to talk of these things constantly (see Deut. 6, 11), and now in a time in history when pen and paper are cheap, we can easily write to aid our remembering.

4

The Heart of Psalm 119

A s we seek, we do not grope in the darkness, but have His light shining in our hearts, enlightening us. We cling to all God has revealed, we seek Him continually once we discover how delightful and true He is. But the God who speaks, revealing all this, does not give it in sound-bites. He has not sanctioned that we all read a devotional book rather than His Word. There are some called to be teachers (and some teach through writing), but they are not to replace Scripture. Rather they teach and clarify as we all come to the Word; they push listeners and readers to the Word, not to themselves. Jesus demands that we come to Him for life or have none at all. In our milk drinking days this seems exciting; everything is new. Many of us hit a 'what now?' phase that stifles and confuses us. Or we hit those dark days in which we really don't know what to read and settle for a bit of some new book, or nothing at all. Reading Psalm 119 is not by any means a 'how to' program. But it is as though this Psalmist's journal was included for us to read, so we could learn from our older brother in the faith, to see his joy, and hear how he engages with God's Word in varying seasons of life.

All Christians need time in the Word to study, to ponder, to meditate, to memorize, to journal and muse, to share with other believers in both teaching and admonishing one another as we ought. We all need time to read large sections, and times to focus in on small sections yet without isolating verses and falling prey to the temptation of proof-texting our own thoughts. We need to read it all, to see the big picture, the unfolding of redemptive history. Without the whole of Scripture, we miss seeing the true character of God. These are all facets of seeking and clinging to the Word. These are all ways to describe our abiding in the Word. As we seek, and abide, we grow into these habits. Abiding in His Word is more than a checklist item of whether I glanced at the text. Engage His Word as the Psalmist did, regularly, and you will not be unfruitful. Let this Psalm encourage your soul in your seeking after, clinging to, and abiding in the God who reveals Himself. The God who has spoken and who delights to give understanding. And pray as this Psalm teaches us, asking 'that I may learn' and please 'teach me!'

Engaging the Word

Many portions of Scripture teach us to love the Lord our God with all our heart, our soul, our mind and our strength, and this Psalm in particular details one's worship beautifully in this way. This worshiper engages his whole being in seeking after and delighting in his God and prayerfully we can grow in this as we study this Psalm. He declares that God's Word is wonderful, and his soul observes it. He declares that God's words grant his mind understanding. He claims to have 'inclined' his heart to carry out fully what God commands (see Psalm 119:112, 129-130). So many verses of this great poem relate the worshipers' heart, soul, mind, or body to the Word, we really cannot grow in our inner being if we try to compartmentalize, or cling too tightly to dualistic tendencies. Heart and mind are not separate, we cannot love Him with head but not heart. We love, or we do not. We abide, or we do not. He has spoken and brought us to life – or we are dead in our sins, without hope, without life, without the ability to know or love Him. Let those of us who know Him, who are known by Him, join James in the work of purifying our hearts from our double-mindedness, that we may draw near, and listen (James 4:8-10).

The first two verses of Psalm 119 are a stunning display of this whole-being devotedness that is our calling. Blessed are those whose body and mind and heart work together to know and love God as He has revealed Himself:

> How blessed are those whose way is blameless,
> Who walk in the law of the LORD.
> How blessed are those who observe His testimonies,
> Who seek Him with all *their* heart.

Walking, that is bodily acting upon His righteous ways. Observing with the senses, thoughtfully engaging the mind to notice how God has created the world, and how His decrees carry out His work. Seeking God with the heart, the seat of emotions and desires, and the place where all our choices and plans are devised. To abide in Him is to keep these together, to be whole, rather than tearing them apart. We are not privileged to choose which ones are for laypeople, and which for the elders and pastors, as though only elders are devoted to God and the rest of us are once a week seekers.

Delight

> Trouble and anguish have come upon me,
> Yet Your commandments are my delight (Psalm 119:143).

This Psalmist knows, and writes about, the ups and downs of life that all of us will face. Trouble and anguish are no stranger to Him, and in the midst of difficult times he chooses to stay in Scripture rather than wallow in self-pity. Introspection, despair, or hiding may seem like appropriate responses to the masses (if we are going to be 'true to our self'), but it is not the helpful or faithful response. Delighting in God's Word is the Psalmist's choice, and proves to be like balm to one in the trenches. Not only are God's commandments His delight (see also verses 47-48), but also the 'testimonies' of the Lord (see verses 24, 111), and God's law (see verses 69-70, 174).

Delighting in all the Scripture available to him, the Psalmist found hope, comfort, direction, and joy. To delight in something requires that we give time and attention to it. If in our seasons of life that seem pleasant, we abide in His Word, we will find our souls' deepest longings spoken to, promises and hope offered, wisdom and answers given, understanding grown and love for God and His glory deepening. Then, when trouble and anguish surround us, we look to what we have written on the tablet of our hearts (see Prov. 3:3) and in our journals, cling to it, and our countenance is lifted. We can choose to look to God rather than only gazing inwardly or focusing on circumstances and then feeling helpless. Our delight can remain with us, and in us, when our delight is in the eternal words of our God.

Rejoice, Sing

> I rejoice at Your word,
> as one who finds great spoil (Psalm 119:162).

Surely we can all imagine winning the lottery, or a long lost relative bequeathing us millions of dollars and an estate to match. We all delight in stories like 'The Little Princess' knowing it would be beyond delightful to have all our needs met, no worries for the future, and extra to spend on frivolous wants and giving to our friends and neighbors. Would finding a stash of pirate treasure bring you more satisfaction than being able to understand Scripture? If we do not sit long in His words, meditating and musing, how could they compete? The world fools us and plasters our hearts so our longings cannot be directed to their proper end, an all-satisfying end.

This Psalmist claims that when persecutions arise, his heart is stayed upon God's words, in awe of them, rather than alarmed at circumstances. This does not happen to one who claims to believe God yet does not abide in His words. This does not mean the Psalmist is wearing rose-colored glasses, unable to comprehend the reality he is living in. He has enemies, they persecute him, they lie about him, they afflict him greatly. Yet he does not blame God or abandon God, for he knows that God is just though these other human beings are practicing injustice. God is good, though not all the people surrounding him are good. God's words are true though people are deceitful. One standing in awe of God through His Word will rejoice at all the understanding the Spirit gives, rejoicing as one whose stocks just shot through the roof, and now retirement is more than fully funded.

Longing, Waiting For

My soul languishes for Your salvation;
I wait for Your word.
My eyes fail with *longing* for Your word ... (Psalm 119:81-82).

From beginning to end, the Psalmist declares many times his longing, his waiting, and his emotional turmoil in these times. The longing at times crushes his soul (see Psalm 119:20). He is not expressing a delighted desire for more, this longing is felt so deeply that he knows his absolute need for more. More knowledge and understanding that can only come from the Lord. Several times his eyes fail with longing. Imagine eyes too tired to stay awake, yet you read more because a deep longing spurs you on. In verse 174, the longing is connected to the delight he has in the Word. He waits for the Word that will revive, that will bring relief, that will bring help. He admits the Lord is his hiding place, and therefore he waits for more. The metaphor of a thirsty being panting for refreshment is used to describe this longing (see Psalm 119:131). In our longing, we are tempted to settle; we grow impatient and make up our own words or listen to easy soothing voices. The Psalmist waits, and pants for the only words that will bring what he needs. We can wait too, and we ought to listen to the deep longings of our souls, panting after His Word, and thereby wait on the Holy Spirit to grant understanding as we read Scripture.

Observe, Behold

Open my eyes that I may behold
wonderful things from Your law (Psalm 119:18).

Beholding and observing were regular occurrences to this Psalmist. He set the Word before himself, and observed, took note, paid attention to what he learned and let it enlighten his view of the reality he lived in. He saw the blessings granted in times of obedience. He claimed to observe God's testimonies, precepts, ordinances, commandments, testimonies, statutes, and law (see Psalm 119:22, 30, 56, 115, 129, 145). In other words, the Psalmist chases after all the words of his God, wanting to know them all, wanting to see their truthfulness play out in his life, wanting the flourishing that stems from obedience to the ways of shalom, properly relating to his King.

Meditate

> Oh how I love Your law!
> It is my meditation all the day (Psalm 119:97).

Our minds are active all day, and this Psalmist has learned how to set his mind rather than letting his mind be ruled by every distraction. He greatly anticipates times when he will be able to meditate for more than a moment, knowing the privilege it is to have such a word and such a time to think upon it (see Psalm 119:148). Developing the habit of meditating on God's Word has proven to help in times of trouble and distress; times when a believer who is not used to being in God's Word would normally rail against the hope and assurance and strength offered therein (see Psalm 119:78). Lies and oppression are no match for our souls when we are saturated in God's Word, having made time to meditate often. This Psalmist mentions meditating on God's precepts and statutes (see Psalm 119:15, 23, 48, 78) but he also spends time meditating on God's wonders (see Psalm 119:27). How often do your interactions with nature, music, math, and science cause you to be in awe of your creator? How often have you read the history of redemption and marveled at the record of it? How often do you read of miracles, whether the parting of the Red Sea or Jordan River, or raising Lazarus from the dead, and just stay there in that story, meditating on the wonder? The wonder of God's power, His compassion, His gentleness, His strength, and all the other aspects of God's character that are revealed in God's wonders?

Trust

The Psalmist asks for the covenant-loyalty-love of the Lord to come to him, and for salvation 'according to Your Word,' because he trusts in the Word of the Lord (see Psalm 119:41-42). His confidence to pray and trust was not from within, it was from the words he had learned and remembered and trusted. Likewise our confidence to persist in prayer would grow if we too abide in His Word and learn to trust Him who is faithful, loyal, loving. A great illustration of a heart that trusts God's Word is found in verses 163-165, wherein he describes the peace that fills him so that he would not stumble. 'Stumble' is not to be understood to mean that life will be easy, but that his heart would not stumble away from the faith, not falter in unbelief. One who trusts God's Word would 'esteem right' all that God has revealed, rather than esteeming falsehood or doubt or doublemindedness (see Psalm 119:128).

Prayers Found Within

There is no self-help found here in this Psalm. The Psalmist was continually asking for strength and help from the Lord. He asked often for reviving, and even for deliverance. He knew his need for God, and truly lived out the belief that God is glorified in our dependence upon Him. He boldly prays 'Remember the word to Your servant, In which You have made me hope ... Your word has revived me' (see Psalm 119:49-50). He knew God's promises, he knew God's abilities, he knew God's faithfulness to carry out His words, and prayed in faith from those words. How would your faith multiply if your prayers echoed this sentiment!

Keeping the Words

Keeping the Word is a concept scattered through this Psalm, a very life-giving activity to the Psalmist. Similarly, Jesus taught His disciples to keep His Word. 'He who has My commandments and keeps them is the one who loves Me; and he who loves Me will be loved by My Father, and I will love him and will disclose Myself to him' (John 14:21). But why not to the world, why only to those who have and keep His Word? Answer, verse 23, ' ... If anyone loves Me, he will keep My word; and My Father will love him, and We will come to him and make Our abode with him' (John 14:23). The mutual abiding assures us of growth in knowledge, and in grace. God speaks and brings us to life, He speaks and we keep those words, He speaks, pouring upon us grace upon grace, pouring rivers of living water into our souls continually. Speaking life into us continually. Jesus will ever be ministering to our souls through His Word, though we in our frantic desire to walk by sight will search for a new image. The logos, the Word came, do we dare demand instead a new form of art, music, incense, euphoria of some sort? Will we listen, keep, remember, and walk in the revealed truth? Keeping, for the Psalmist, is done with the whole heart, diligently, and leads to an experience of God's presence that will not be had apart from His Word. To appreciate this, take some time to meander through these verses: 119:4, 8, 16, 34, 44, 52, 55, 83, 87, 93, 110, 141, 168, and 176.

Taking Time

Slowly reading Psalm 119, taking note of the verbs, unfolds the reality that *all* believers need times in which to observe, to seek, to keep and remember, to rejoice in, to long for and wait for, to trust, to meditate on, to cling to, to sing out of, to treasure and delight in, to be in awe of, to learn, and to walk (and run) in God's Word. The Psalmist delights in having grown deeper in knowledge than his teachers because of his love for and engagement with the Word. Let this Psalm fill you with delight at the same prospect. Engage, do not shy away. This life of abiding is for you beloved, not just your teachers, elders, pastors and shepherds. You are not too busy for this, your time here on earth is too important *not* to do this. This is the way of abiding in God's Word, engaging with it fully. Abide, and the vine will make you a fruitful branch.

Practices

Commit to reading this Psalm at least twice per year, praying as the Psalmist did: 'open my eyes, that I may behold wonderful things from Your law' (Psalm 119:18). Plan these times as a special time to 'kindle afresh' (2 Tim. 1:6) your love for His Word, your desire to seek Him, your desire to learn from Him, your zeal to use this treasure for His glory, and to seek His grace as you grow in knowledge.

Spend some time thinking through how you can intentionally spend time interacting with the Word as the Psalmist did. Discipline yourself to set daily, weekly, and seasonal goals. God's love is intentional, yours can be too. How should you be in the Word daily? When during the week can you set aside time for deeper study? Will your daily goals be morning and evening? Will your Sunday include more time for worshiping as you read? Revisit your goals in a year, to see if you can notice whether the Spirit of discipline and sound mind has helped you in this.

5

Refuge and Dwelling Place

In seeking with our whole being we find the Lord. In clinging we remember and internalize all of the truth, goodness and beauty He reveals. And we find one of the most satisfying promises we have to cling to, one that we recognize as fulfilled in Christ and continuing for all eternity; the promise to be our dwelling place, and to dwell among and in us. These Old Testament passages are a necessary background for our understanding of abiding; they are the proper foundation. God's desire has always been to dwell with us, and for us to dwell in Him. Many wonderful books have been written on this, here we will only touch on some promises and their fulfillment, and how our hearts are enlarged when we meditate on this. People were never meant to feel alone, we were created for community, to be in this relationship of mutual dwelling together. We were never meant to hunger and thirst for safety, refreshment, comfort, and love as though we were languishing in a desert. God is the satisfaction of all the hunger and thirst we experience. We were created anew in Christ, that we may find our home in Him, abide in Him, and He in us.

We will start by looking at Christ as the fulfillment. We live in a time when Christ, having come in the fullness of times, proved to be all of this for us. The Apostle John began his telling of the Gospel by showing Christ as the fulfillment:

> And the Word became flesh, and dwelt among us, and we saw His glory, glory as of the only begotten from the Father, full of grace and truth. No one has seen God at any time; the only begotten God who is in the bosom of the Father, He has explained *Him* (John 1:14, 18).

He explained, He made manifest, He led God out to be seen. And God was seen to be dwelling among His people, calling them to Himself, promising to be the source of life, the light, the way, the I am. This was too much for many to accept, but it was not too much for Him to offer. He was calling His own deep into the longed-for fellowship and doing all things necessary to make it possible. We needed redemption, reconciliation, cleansing and Jesus did it. While among us, He accomplished it and now the promise is that He will make us stand, will complete the work begun in us, and will present us to God, 'blameless with great joy' (see Jude 24) when He brings us home. Then we will dwell with Him fully.

Ultimate Desire

In this post-Genesis 3 world, a world saturated with sin and brokenness, our souls crave a place to rest, to hide, to find shelter from the heat and the storms of life, and to find security. What we are given is not a place, but a person and His all-encompassing embrace.

> [A Prayer of Moses the man of God]
> Lord, You have been our dwelling place [or hiding place] in all generations. Before the mountains were born
> Or You gave birth to the earth and the world,
> Even from everlasting to everlasting You are God (Psalm 90:1-2).

> He who dwells in the shelter of the Most High
> Will abide in the shadow of the Almighty.
> I will say to the LORD, 'My refuge and my fortress,
> My God, in whom I trust!' (Psalm 91:1-2).

Dwelling with the LORD, in the Lord, was both the heart's cry and ultimate comfort these Psalmists delighted in. This relationship is indeed our soul's ultimate desire and satisfaction. The ability to enjoy it fully is not yet ours, but the Spirit was given that we might freely know the things that are ours in Christ, though they are difficult to imagine (see 1 Cor. 2:9-13).

While facing sin, and desiring restoration, David's prayer in this next Psalm displays a posture of leaning further into the Lord, rather than running away or pretending. He knew the pain of hiding from the Lord, conversely David knew that in hiding in the Lord he would find joy, and counsel, and steadfast love. His prayer teaches us that the truly godly action in these times is to repent, own up to our sin and hide in Christ, rather than hide from Him as Adam did.

> I acknowledged my sin to You, and my iniquity I did not hide;
> … and You forgave the guilt of my sin.
> Therefore, let everyone who is godly pray to You in a time when You may be found …
> You are my hiding place;
> You preserve me from trouble;
> You surround me with songs of deliverance (Psalm 32:5-7).

Imagine those songs, beloved! God's deliverance and nearness are also promised to us in Psalm 34. 'None of those who take refuge in Him will be condemned' (verse 22). If God is your refuge, the safety is eternal. The redemption is eternal. The condemnation fell on Christ on the cross, and it is finished. This reassurance is echoed in Romans 8. As we struggle with sin or walking away, call this to mind – even then we will not be condemned, Christ will keep you.

It is worth pausing here to meditate on Isaiah 32:2, a verse intended to point us to our all sufficient Redeemer, who is our Prophet, Priest and King. He rules righteously both in our hearts, and in His entire world. He is our refuge, and our shelter. We long to hide and He bids us to hide in Him. Our Redeemer is a stream in a dry country; we thirst and find a source that never runs dry. Streams of living water pouring into our thirsty souls (see also John 4:13-14; 7:37-38). We grow weary and long for rest, for comfort, for aid. We find our Rock to provide all of this in the vast and lifeless desert we walk through.

God gave the designs for the tabernacle and the temple; within was a place where God's glory would dwell. We have come to understand this as the sanctuary. Israel was taught to treat God as holy, and therefore not to enter the sanctuary; our sinful self cannot be in the presence of God's holiness and glory. But all of redemptive history was working toward the time when the veil separating us from God's holiness would be torn, when Christ would be the way for us to dwell in the presence of God's glory. God hints at this great work of reconciliation and cleansing:

> My dwelling place also will be with them; and I will be their God, and they will be My people. And the nations will know that I am the Lord who sanctifies Israel, when My sanctuary is in their midst forever (Ezek. 37:27-28).

His desire from all eternity was for His people to be with Him. His sanctuary would not be separate, but in our midst. Forever. God has long desired to draw us into this abiding relationship, and He is glorified in working out this plan in and amongst us.

Temple and Tabernacle as Shadow

Just as God walked in the cool of the evening with Adam and Eve, so God's desire has always been to be with His people whom He created for His own glory. Hebrews tells us that the tabernacle and temple were the shadows of Christ to come, copies of the realities in heaven. When God gave instructions concerning the tabernacle and the temple, all Israel knew this would be the place where God's glory would dwell among them. What an awesome thing, a plan that pointed to Christ. When Christ came, He claimed that the temple of His body would die and be raised in three days. In Christ the fullness of Deity dwelt. He was not partly God, or part of His former self. When He came to dwell among mankind Jesus was fully God, fully the Son that He has always been, is and ever will be. He had put on flesh but did not cease to be Himself. And so God 'tabernacled' among us, or dwelt among us.

When the Psalmist prayed 'We have thought on Your [covenant-loyalty-love], O God, in the midst of Your temple' he was expressing what our prayers can be (see Psalm 48:9). To worship in spirit and truth, to abide in Him, we must think upon God's steadfast, loyal, redeeming love. And we must let these thoughts be directed by God's Word, and let these thoughts lead us to His temple, that is, consciously into God's presence.

Christ the Reality

As you meditate upon Christ as your dwelling place and your temple, the book of Hebrews will become more and more dear. Therein you will see the Old Covenant worship regulations that were symbolic, and that could not make us perfect (see Heb. 9:9). The Old Covenant sacrifices described could only cleanse the flesh, not a person's conscience (see Heb. 9:13-14). The tabernacle, the sacrifices, and the ceremony were all shadows, pointing toward the reality; they could not make any of God's worshipers clean or perfect (see Heb. 10:1). They serve a glorious purpose, God's law was not a mistake, and is not to be abhorred. Rather, we see the old for what it is, and we delight in the new that has come in Christ. The High Priest of the New Covenant has perfected us for all time (see Heb. 10:14). We don't feel it now, we battle with contrary inner desires, fight with sin, and trudge through the tribulations this world offers us. Yet none of that is our ultimate reality. Christ is the way, and in Him we put off the old self daily, and we abide, we rest. This New Covenant, one of grace alone, provides us with the perfect sacrifice, the perfect mediator, and complete cleansing. We rest, and cease striving, knowing He satisfied all of the law's demands and set us free.

'Sacrifice and offering You have not desired' (Heb. 10:5), instead they were pointers to our need for something greater. We are incapable of living perfectly righteously, we need Christ's righteousness. Hebrews describes Christ's coming as a time of reformation. He takes away the first to establish the second; the shadows are gone, the light has come (see Heb. 9:8–10:14). The offering of Christ's body is sufficient, once for all, never to be repeated, and now by this one offering we are assured of our place in His kingdom. We can rest in that knowledge, abiding in Him for our life moment by moment.

Studying Hebrews 9–10:18 will grant us confidence to enter God's presence continually. We need not wait as in the Old Covenant for the high priest to enter once a year, nor for a prophet to speak God's Word. Our great high priest sits enthroned, having completed our redemption. We now 'draw near with a sincere heart in full assurance of faith' (Heb. 10:22). He cleanses our hearts and minds from impurities, that we may hear and trust His words, and fills us with the endurance to cling to our true hope and to live in 'the simplicity and purity *of devotion* to Christ' (2 Cor. 11:3). That endurance is crucial, because sometimes we feel our imperfections acutely and wonder if we should pray, or wonder what to read, or whether we can read Scripture. Draw near, beloved. His love is everlasting, His grace and mercy are for you.

Abiding and Rest

How does Jesus reform our view of the Sabbath? Exodus 20 commands us to do or not do certain things in keeping the Sabbath holy. Isaiah 58 refines this by teaching that to keep it holy we must find the Sabbath to be a delight. The Hebrew word for delight there signifies to be of dainty habit, be pampered, to be happy about, take exquisite delight, to make merry over, make sport of. Jesus teaches that the Sabbath is for man, not the other way around. As we abide in Him, we rest. Thus in keeping the Sabbath holy it is still a time of rest, refreshment, repose, recreation, freedom, feasting, worship, celebration, remembrance, hope, and delight. We keep it holy primarily by setting aside things that distract us from consciously abiding. We turn away from activities and hobbies and work that belong to the other six days, activities that do not usher our souls into flourishing rest. The Sabbath is a sign, and a gift. It meets some needs and desires now, and it points us to our future rest, our eternal life, our abundant life that begins now, and our utter dependence on Him who made us perfect.

Christ did not take away the Sabbath rest when He fulfilled the law for us, but has transformed it. He abolished the ceremonial portions and freed us from striving for a righteousness we cannot attain. We rest, but we do not merely take a day off from typical work. This is to be a culmination or celebration of our continual resting in Him. We set aside a day to bask in our soul's true delights, and we do not forsake gathering that we might enjoy this rest together. We work six days, but we gather in our time off to worship, grow, and rejoice together that our full rest is surely ahead.

We Are the Temple Now

As the time to be crucified drew near, Jesus taught His disciples that it was better for Him to leave so that the Spirit could be sent to dwell in God's people in a way that Jesus was not doing. The Father would send the Spirit, and in so doing God's people would become God's temple. He would be dwelling in them, anointing them, teaching them, drawing them further into an ever-abiding fellowship.

This temple imagery does not stop there, for Paul taught that both believers, and local churches (where two or more were gathered), are the temple:

> … For we are the temple of the living God; just as God said,
> 'I will dwell in them and walk among them;
> and I will be their God, and they shall be My people.
> And I will be a father to you,
> And you shall be sons and daughters to Me,'
> Says the Lord Almighty (2 Cor. 6:16, 18).

And as has always been the case, God would protect His people. And now He would protect His new temple, the church:

> Do you not know that you are a temple of God and that the Spirit of God dwells in you? If any man destroys the temple of God, God will destroy him, for the temple of God is holy, and that is what you are (1 Cor. 3:16-17).

This 'you' is plural, collectively they are the church, the temple of the living God. Not only does God dwell in us, He has given us belonging amongst His people. We are not alone, we belong. We are a part. Does this not speak to the deepest of our soul's cries, and needs? To know that God has created us for His glory, and is our refuge, our hiding place, our dwelling place. And there we are, with God abiding in us, in His people. Together, amongst sisters and brothers, we are members of Christ's body. When the desire to run away is bubbling up within you, call this to mind. God stopped at nothing to make this a reality, that He would dwell in you, abide in you and you in Him. And to create a community of like-minded abiding-in-Him people with whom you can walk through these sojourning days.

Filled

Of Christ's fullness we have received. Therefore, we come near to God, we draw near with confidence. Daily, moment by moment, with reverence and awe, without fear or doubt. As the first temple built was filled with God's glory, so He fills us, and dwells in us. We need not fear to draw near to the one who has made His abode in us. The veil was torn after Christ was crucified to display the reformation He brought about. The old is passing away, the new has come, and we now worship in spirit and truth rather than in a prescribed place. We draw near in full assurance, we stand firm in the faith, by the working of the Holy Spirit in us. None could enter that first temple to draw near to God's dwelling place, but now we are God's dwelling place because of Christ's finished work. Sin separated mankind from God's presence, His magnificent glory would not be tarnished by sin. In Christ, God's justice has been satisfied on our behalf, we are now free. Free from fear, from sin's power, from the law's decrees against us. Free to abide, to draw near, to live a life filled by His Spirit rather than any other pseudo life-source (See Eph. 3:11-21).

We do not need the fullness of God 'and' any other thing. The fullness dwelt in Christ, and He now dwells in us. In Christ we are filled, we are made complete. Complete. Nothing else completes us. In Christ alone we are free to obey, to choose what is good, knowing we are not attempting to earn redemption. Redemption is complete, our vocations are therefore done for God's glory, not to make something of ourselves. We love and serve and seek to lead quiet lives, rather than trying to find identity or meaning or purpose in the world, outside of Christ (thus destroying the purity and simplicity of the life He has given us). We are free to rest in who we are as hidden in Christ, while the world struggles to find themselves and prove their worth.

Because we are filled, we are not shaken, we overcome, we endure, we persevere. We live in wonder of our great God, and in the hope He gives us. Our rock dwells in us, His strength and steadfastness are ever available to us. He is more clearly the fountainhead of all we long for and need, and we gaze nowhere else, but upon Him.

Practices

Find a few hymns or spiritual songs that preach this idea to your soul, and spend a season memorizing them. Singing lifts our souls, lifts our emotional wellbeing, and is a most useful way to remind ourselves of truth.

Spend a season journaling through the verses from this chapter (among others you find in your times studying the Word) that teach about the tabernacle, the temple, Jesus' physical body as the temple, believers as the temple, the church as the temple. Let this shape your theology as you think about 'the holy catholic church' and the 'fellowship of the saints' and of God's desire for unbroken fellowship with you.

Commit Psalm 119:114 to memory: 'You are my hiding place and my shield; I wait for Your word.'

Keep it in mind, cling to this verse, pray through this verse, and call this verse to mind, that it is not a new word you wait for. The Scriptures are sufficient, the Word already given is what you wait for. You wait to sense His nearness, to have the Spirit massage it into your heart, to see how it lightens your path, to find therein the comfort and joy God intends to give.

Journal through these passages: Psalm 40:6-11, Hosea 6:6, 1 Samuel 15:22, Isaiah 1:11-14, Matthew 9:13 and 12:7. Ponder the greatness of Christ's sacrifice, His life, and His drawing you near. What do these passages lead us to delight in? Commit to delighting in what pleases God most.

6

Hope

True hope is given to us by God and this hope never disappoints. It is sure and steadfast, and our experience of it grows as we abide. Hope is exciting to God's children and motivates us when our hearts begin to fail. We do not hope for earthly things, that is a complete misuse of the Word. We hope for the city to come, for the promises belonging to the new heavens and the new earth, for the time when He will have finished making all things new. We hope for His eternal redemption won for us on the cross. Our hope is directed toward Jesus, the perfect mediator of the New Covenant (see Heb. 9:10-12). We trust that Jesus really has gone to prepare a place for us and will come back to take us home. He has removed the veil and we see dimly now, as we wait for the time when we will see Him as He really is (2 Cor. 3:12-18).

In hope, we seek the city that is to come, we anticipate the beauty and perfection of our future home, we wait with expectant patience. The Old Testament prophets spoke often, revealing glimpses of this heavenly home. The New Testament Epistles quite often draw us to ponder those glimpses. Sometimes believers set this aside as 'not useful' as though God created us only for pragmatic endeavors.

But can any acting in faith happen apart from looking to Him, gazing at Him seated on His throne? As often as the Scriptures direct our gaze heavenward in hope, so we ought to trust that this is indeed a good and necessary habit to cultivate. Directing our thoughts, our affections, and our energy toward what lies ahead, the future He has promised. We hope for what we have not seen. Our resurrected Lord is faithful and will fulfill His promise to take us home. And that home will be beyond our wildest imagination.

He Goads Us On

What does hope do within us as we set our gaze expectantly upon Christ, anticipating His return? As we look to find our life hidden in Him? This exercise of hope is our proper motivation, and therefore more deeply pragmatic than any to-do list or human program for becoming Christlike. Remember that feeling as a child, on the night before Christmas? Or the night before going to camp, or going on vacation? Those sorts of experiences ought to be seen as a foretaste. As adults, we hope, and are not disappointed. All those expectations for our heavenly home that we read about in Scripture, for the new heavens and new earth, will prove true.

We are prone in this culture to separate what is useful and what is extraneous. Physical tasks become more highly prized than mental and emotional engagements. As there is nothing new, so Paul was led to write to both the Ephesians and the Colossians about this same misplaced valuation. Paul focused on our inheritance, on where Jesus currently is, what Jesus is currently doing, and how our true selves are hidden there with Christ. What is Jesus' current posture toward us? What are His thoughts toward us? We are asked over and over to ponder heaven. So, do you? Are you on pilgrimage here, awaiting your true home or are you at home here wondering what could possibly be real about heaven, focusing instead on finding immediate comfort? If we are focused on immediate comfort, do we really care for others or usher His kingdom in? God goads us on in our ministry of reconciliation as we are enraptured with the hope set before us. Hope fuels us to live in this world knowing it is not all there is. We can store up treasures in heaven because we know our possessions here are fleeting. This world will not last, it is passing away, but our heavenly home is everlasting. This world will be shaken, but our citizenship is in the unshakable kingdom (see Heb. 12:18-29). This hope then keeps us from focusing on anything earthly as ultimate, as final, or as the worthiest goal of our life. Therefore, we work here, engage in culture or business or leisure here, without being defined or disheartened by it.

Pondering what the prophets and apostles have written will change how you walk through trials. Thinking about our inheritance and storing up heavenly treasures will change the way you meet suffering, affliction, and difficulties. For one who has never pondered the hope of Christ that is now ours, the Word of God is shunned during times of suffering. Some may not take to heart the encouragement found in Scriptures, and will turn away, sometimes in anger, from a brother who offers a glimpse of hope.

But to the one who lingers over these passages, to whom the Spirit has given understanding, the experience is different. To that one God's Word, whether read or spoken by a brother or sister in Christ, brings revival. His Word of hope brings comfort and lifts our eyes away from focusing on our present suffering to looking at deeper truth and eternal stores of life and peace. The Lord is never far away, even in these times. He is using them to produce a weight of glory (go back to 2 Cor. 4) far beyond the capabilities of our finite mind to understand. The most glorious being does not leave us during these times, nor has He promised we would live sheltered from them. Each one of us will walk through times when Joseph's words ring true: though this situation is embedded in the circumstances of an evil world, it is meant by God for ultimate (soul) good, and for God's glory (Gen. 50:20 ref).

Our only hope then is not from within, not from earthly circumstances or voices, but is set upon God as revealed in His Word. We wait eagerly and patiently for our true hope (see Rom. 8:18-25). We join the Psalmist who waits for God's Word. God will act, His power will remain unmatched. 'I wait for the LORD, my soul does wait, and in His Word do I hope' (Psalm 130:5). We do not look for the power of God's acting on our behalf apart from His Word. Like the Thessalonians, we hear the Word as it is delivered, in power, accompanied by the Holy Spirit, and with belief (see 1 Thess. 1:5).

Hope and Joy

The source of Jesus' joy was in His being in the Father, and He calls us into this joy. He told His disciples that all He had spoken to them, which the Spirit would remind them of, was all so that His own joy would fill them (see John 17). Jesus was not giving them a false hope of easy times in their immediate earthly future. His joy is not merely a time of lighthearted laughter. Jesus was promising to fill them with joy in the midst of earthly tribulations. The joy and peace He promised was tied to the glory He desires to draw us into. Studying John 17 greatly influences a deeper understanding of Paul's teaching to the Colossians on the 'hope of glory' in chapter three of that Epistle. Preach to your own soul then, that in the midst of any vocation, any tribulation, and even amidst difficult dark days, we have an unchanging hope of glory.

> The glory which You have given Me I have given to them, that they may be one, just as We are one; I in them and You in Me, that they may be perfected in unity … (John 17:22-23a).

There is a measure of glory given to us, His church, now. This glory, with its source in the Trinity, is given to the church for the experiencing of unity. Gazing upon our Lord we delight in His glory, in His promise of mutual abiding and so delight in this calling. Gazing upon our own agendas destroys this unity. It is our sinful flesh that ruins unity, not a mere difference of opinion. Abiding in His words clarifies His desires for us, but our disunity testifies to our lack of delight in His Word, and the affections we have set upon earthly things and ideals.

He bore the cross with perfect joy set before Him (Heb. 12:2), so we walk through the tribulations of this earthly life with that very joy offered to us. We will walk with this joy even through the tribulation of disunity or isolation amongst the church. May He fill you with all joy and peace as you believe, but not as you grasp for earthly substitutes (see Rom. 15:13).

Boasting in Hope

Hebrews 3 and 4 instructs the church that in the midst of earthly strife and tribulation, we all ought to hold fast to several things:our confidence, the boast of our hope, our assurance, and our confession (see Heb. 3:6; 3:14; 4:14). Holding fast to these has great benefit for our hearts and minds as we endure and exult in our daily affairs. Even when our daily affairs include struggles with sin, with contrary worldviews, or with everything raising itself up against Christ, our hope is sure and steadfast.

Nothing can be hidden from God's sight, no one can hide from the creator and sustainer of all life. Yet we do not fear when we read of the Spirit wielding His two-edged sword, piercing and cutting, getting at every thought of our hearts and minds. Rather we hold fast remembering that nothing can separate us from His love, not even our sin (which He has redeemed us from) or our wayward thinking. This sword cuts away all that is flesh, all that is opposed to God's glory. Therefore, we do not fear, we know this chastening, or this pruning, will be for our good and His glory. Think of what fruit can come after the branch (that is you, beloved) has had all the dead parts cut away!

What is our confidence, then? That Christ, who was tempted and suffered and yet did not sin, ' … is able to come to the aid of those who are tempted' (Heb. 2:18). Our high priest was faithful to His Father and will be faithful to help us. '… Christ *was faithful* as a Son over His house–whose house we are …' (Heb. 3:6). Our confidence is in our union with Christ, knowing our lives are hidden in Him, finding all we need in and from Him alone. We are His, and of this we are confident, therefore we are strengthened for our daily lives as we cling to this reality, or as we '… hold fast our confidence …' (Heb. 3:6).

Next we hear of holding fast to the '… boast of our hope firm until the end …' (Heb. 3:6). We do not keep our hope hidden, we boast in it, daily boasting until Jesus returns or takes us home. Till the end. Boasting of this hope, after basking in it. Time meditating and journaling regularly through Hebrews 10:34b–11:40 will help you grow in this. Praying through the Psalms will give voice to your boast. When you have grasped that you really do have much better possessions in heaven than here, your affections and emotions and thought patterns will be shaped to match, and your actions will follow. You will work for that heavenly treasure rather than for a temporal treasure which perishes. You will love as He did, and love what He did. You will value the pleasures at God's right hand over the passing pleasures of this world. Your use of time, your attitude toward money, and your emotional responses to upsets will change as your affections come in line with Christ's. And they will come in line, as you bask in and boast of your hope. Christ is coming again, let us join the throng who eagerly await Him, our confidence lies therein.

We also hold fast to our assurance; we hold fast to what we have heard and we know that He will be faithful to all He has promised. We draw near in this assurance, knowing Jesus covers us with His blood, and His righteousness. Our assurance is rooted in Christ, through whom we draw near. Our mediator assures us of our continuance and endurance because of His constant ministry of intercession (Heb. 7:25). We need never make any sacrifice, His is sufficient. We need never add to His work, it was a permanent solution and our redemption is accomplished once for all time. This assurance propels us to walk in His love, and in His ways, bearing much fruit.

> And we desire that each one of you show the same diligence so as to realize the full assurance of hope until the end, so that you will not be sluggish, but imitators of those who through faith and patience inherit the promises (Heb. 6:11-12).

Our assurance is rooted in His ability, His faithfulness, His love, and His unchanging nature. Our diligence is not a striving. We realize our full assurance by finding it in Him, not by making it. Our diligence is not self-effort, but rather a faith that works as described in James 2. We boast in our hope, and this energizes our faith which in turn shows itself through our words and deeds.

The Good Confession

Finally, the author of Hebrews mentions holding fast to one's confession (see Heb. 4:14). What was your confession? What did you confess? Romans 10 is a good starting point to understand what the beginning of our confession is. We confess who Jesus is, and who He is for us. This is not all we confess though, as though a one-liner were the sum of our faith.

> Fight the good fight of faith; take hold of the eternal life to which you were called, and you made the good confession in the presence of many witnesses. I charge you in the presence of God, who gives life to all things, and of Christ Jesus, who testified the good confession before Pontius Pilate (1 Tim. 6:12-13).

What did Christ Jesus confess? That He is God, one with the Father, and the King of a kingdom that is not of this world (see John 18:28–19:15) who has power even over this decision of Pilate's to crucify Him. Do we confess His power? His sovereign rule? His ability to give life, to be the life? What do we confess? And has our confession grown? God has us on a life-long journey of growing in wisdom and knowledge, of knowing Him more and delighting in Him more truly. Our confession grows deeper as our knowledge of God does. Our joy radiates more purely with this growth, and we can proclaim more and more of His excellencies.

It has tempted some in every generation to aspire only to hold to the basics, leaving all the deep knowledge of our God to our pastors or elders. Our confession was only the beginning of the journey and our life of abiding cannot be stagnant. A stagnant moment points us to our need. 'By this time you ought to be teachers ...' (Heb. 5:12). Christ's desire is ever to build us up, to be formed in us, to see us filled with passion according to a true knowledge of Him, to see us act in faith as one in His kingdom of priests (see Rom. 10:2-3 for a picture of false passion; Titus 2:11-14 for a picture of the godly passion; and Rev. 1:5-6 concerning the kingdom).

Boasting in your hope makes life richer and fuller. It is part of how we fight the good fight of faith, how we hold fast and cling to our Lord. To boast in our hope, we must first bask in it. We are diligent and zealous now, knowing eternal rest is laid up for us in heaven, knowing our assurance, our confidence, and our hope is ultimate. The passing things of this world will no longer hold sway over us when our eyes are fixed on Christ and we hold fast (see 1 Cor. 7:29-31). We do not cling to what is passing away. We cling to reality, not shadow. We too can endure during the time of our sojourning in this world, '...as seeing Him who is unseen' (Heb. 11:27). God promises to be preparing an 'eternal weight of glory' for us 'while' we look at that which is unseen, the hoped for fulfillment of our heavenly home, of living forever in the presence of our Lord and Savior (see 2 Cor. 4:16-18).

Practices
Journal through Romans 5:1-5, and James 1:1-4, 12. Slow down, muse upon each word. Are you merely enduring or are you also exulting in tribulation, and thus in hope? Ponder the difference, and how your whole person is involved and impacted.

Colossians 3:2 would have us regularly set aside time to 'Set your minds on things above ...' What Old Testament passages inform our pondering of heaven? What New Testament passages? Keep in mind that no eye has seen, nor ear heard, and all will be better than we can imagine! If you begin this habit of grace by putting time on your calendar, setting it aside and honoring it, you will build up a reservoir in your soul. You will reach a point at which you no longer have to schedule this habit, it will become a feast you long for, a drink of cold water on a hot sweaty day. You will find that your daily thoughts turn there when you have this reservoir. Then to set your minds will not always be reading the Scriptures, but will be a remembering, a musing, a delightful turning of thoughts.

Pick up a copy of John Bunyan's *Pilgrim's Progress*, an allegory of the Christian life. As you read, take note of the role of Hope the character in the lives of the various pilgrims.

True encouragement is this: knowing Christ in me, the hope of glory! Relate this verse found in the larger passage of Colossians 1:24–2:3 to 1 Corinthians 2:10-16, and 2 Peter 1:19 The Spirit will teach you what the carnal mind cannot know, a true knowledge of Christ Himself, in whom are hidden all the treasures your heart really longs for, including your heavenly inheritance. But He will not teach you apart from His Word, so read, study, journal, think, and do all this while praying without ceasing.

Listen to, read, and sing often through the hymn titled 'The Sands of Time are Sinking' also known as 'Emmanuel's Land.'[1] Memorizing hymns with good theology, scriptural phrases, and memorable tunes will lift your gaze heavenward and enlarge your heart as you worship. This one in particular will focus your thoughts and affections on the hope you ought to boast in.

---

1. 'The Sands of Time are Sinking', Author: Samuel Rutherford; Author: A. R. Cousin (1857)

7

Renewal

Believers are called to have renewed minds, a call which has both passive and active aspects. Actively we seek, we cling, we remember, we grow in knowledge, we believe. But God does the renewing. We present ourselves to God, we receive renewal. He has created us anew and will renew us to a 'true knowledge' and to our true self.

> ... if indeed you have heard Him and have been taught in Him, just as truth is in Jesus, that, in reference to your former manner of life, you lay aside the old self, which is being corrupted in accordance with the lusts of deceit, and that you be renewed in the spirit of your mind, and put on the new self, which in the likeness of God has been created in righteousness and holiness of the truth (Eph. 4:21-24).

> ... since you laid aside the old self with its evil practices, and have put on the new self who is being renewed to a true knowledge according to the image of the One who created him (Col. 3:9b-10).

Though our outward man is suffering the effects of a sin saturated world, we are no longer inwardly decaying.

Though Adam and Eve thought they would gain a knowledge as full as God's, their sin would actually preclude all mankind from a fullness of truth apart from redemption. Rather than continuing in ignorance and inward decay, we are renewed day by day (see 2 Cor. 4:7-18). Every morning that we awake in this world, we turn to God for this work. Unless He renews us inwardly, we will wither away. The vine is a constant source of renewal for all the branches that abide, that remain, that drink their fill. He will bring this work to completion, but not on this earth. Here we die daily, we wait on the Lord daily, we are renewed by Him daily. And one day, we will truly be like Him (1 John 3:1-3). Adam and Eve tried to have the knowledge of good and evil so as to be like God, to live without coming to Him. They experienced the shame and misery immediately, and we live in that state until God renews us. As we abide in Him, He renews our minds. The true source of goodness, and truth is available for us. Knowing God is so much richer than the knowledge given to Adam and Eve as they ate the fruit of the forbidden tree. Daily we need this renewal in our own minds, that we would delight in Him rather than idolize our own separate knowledge.

Diligence

Renewal is not a magical thing that catches us by surprise. Renewal is promised, and we look to Him who is faithful, expecting Him to grant it. Renewal eludes us when our emotions or ill reasoning ensnare us. Our imaginations are far too small. Where the Lord would have us look to Him for help and strength and passion and guidance, we fall short and look instead at our circumstances, our repetitive thoughts (which are never as high as His), our shortcomings. We feel stuck in our patterns of sin and doubt. If we can push through and lay down the old self with its old patterns, looking to Christ all the while, we will be renewed in heart, mind, and soul.

Imagine for a moment you are on a team (pick a sport) and your coach has scheduled practice several times each week. At each practice he has the team running through drills, over and over, the same movements and the same patterns. Eventually these movements become easier, flow easier, and even quicker. These habitual movements and drills have caused your brain and other muscles to form a pathway of doing this sport, this game. Now the game can be played with great joy, speed, and accuracy. But how was the first practice? It is so with math, with learning a new language, a new hobby or sport. Much like these activities that involve the physical, the mental and the emotional aspects of our life, so in our spiritual renewal we must be diligent in all aspects to put off and put on. It will start small, you will need to run many drills, practicing often before you notice new pathways have formed in your brain, and that those ways are smooth, joyful, commonplace. Be devoted to prayer, fellowship, studying God's Word, meditating on His Word, corporate worship, and serving. And soon enough you start to see the fruitfulness that accompanies abiding in Him. Be devoted by sitting at His feet, eager to listen, eager for the Lord to enter in, to dwell in your heart through faith, showing Himself powerful as He works in you (see Eph.3:14-21).

Growing in Grace and Knowledge

Renewal includes growth. True Christians will not remain stagnant as the Spirit who dwells in them yearns to draw them ever closer, as He will. We ought not be surprised when Peter commands his audience to grow in grace and knowledge. This is not an imperative only for those who seem more easily bent toward contemplation, rather it is for all who are in Christ. To abide in Him means to abide in His Word and thereby be renewed in heart and mind and experience growth. As the spirit of your mind is renewed, your whole being enjoys the refreshing, and faith becomes active, showing itself fruitful, zealous even (see Titus 2:14). We manifest the truth not by trying really hard, but by sitting with Jesus. We gaze, we present ourselves, we listen. And in so doing He brings renewal, manifests Himself more deeply, and refreshes us as the spring rains refresh the earth.

We are commanded to be renewed, so that in body, soul, mind and heart we can submit to God. This renewal brings wholeness, so that one faculty will not rule as a god over the others. 'Be renewed' is passive; God ultimately renews. In the obedience of faith, we fulfill our calling to be renewed by setting our minds:

> For those who are according to the flesh set their minds on the things of the flesh, but those who are according to the Spirit, the things of the Spirit. For the mind set on the flesh is death, but the mind set on the Spirit is life and peace (Rom. 8:5-6).

We set our minds on the Spirit by prayerfully engaging with Scripture. Focusing, observing, and meditating on Scripture, which we are told is the sword of the Spirit. James tells us to receive the Word implanted; we are at the receiving end of God's work. We prayerfully read, asking for wisdom and understanding, remembering that the Spirit wields this powerful sword which pierces and cuts away whatever is of the flesh rather than of His Spirit.

A Renewed Conscience

We also present ourselves to be renewed as we set our minds and affections on Christ, who alone has the power to cleanse the conscience. Have you ever wondered what has built up and fed your conscience prior to your union with Christ? What voices did you listen to, cling to, believe? Which of those are contrary to the Word?

We come to Christ for cleansing, for renewal, and are then able to come boldly and stand in His righteousness. With a cleansed conscience, the contrary voices have lost their power to direct our way, and the voices of condemnation have lost their power to discourage. With a cleansed conscience we can serve God, living for His glory, basking in His grace, and listening to the voice of our maker, redeemer, sustainer, lover and friend.

We are very active in the setting of our minds, and we receive the blessing of a renewed heart, soul, mind and body. We set our minds on the Spirit, and thus enjoy God's life and peace (Rom. 8:6). This does not mean we no longer face the deterioration so prevalent in this world. His renewal is not a shield from reality. Glory awaits, meanwhile we are sojourning here, in these tents (2 Cor. 5:1-5). Whenever we grow weary, we turn toward His cross, setting our minds purposefully. We walk here in this world, but our minds are set on Christ above. We live out our earthly days knowing none of this is ultimate. Our renewed minds do not listen to the condemnation of the old man with its fleshly conscience, but to the cleansed conscience that reminds us 'He is your righteousness.' We are more fully human, more fully the selves we were designed and created to be when we walk by faith, renewed in our minds to this true knowledge. If our knowledge ends with merely what we see, despair sets in. Anxiety follows close behind. Faith weakens. And our prayer life becomes a list of physical needs.

Wonder, Awe

We find renewal in being overwhelmed by wonder at the glory, the love, the beauty, the power, and the majesty of

God as revealed in His Word, and His works (pause here to read Psalm 111). We abide in God's Word to have His perspective, to view our circumstances with the mind of Christ rather than an earthly perspective.

It is in God's nature to carry out this work of renewal, as you'll find in studying Isaiah 57:15; 40:28-29; 45:6-8; and Jeremiah 31:25. These verses anticipate that as we abide in Christ we will be overwhelmed by the glory of God! To ponder God's character, to meditate on verses revealing God's desires for and delight in His people, will bring about a renewed mind and heart and soul. Thinking upon God's sovereignty and His desire to revive ushers us into worship and draws us deeper into God's love and glory.

This renewal invites us to cast away any broken cisterns we've been drinking from, to drink only from the streams of living water that never run out, never grow stale or stagnant, never breed disease or fail to satisfy our thirst. We drink from the fountain of life and are filled, empowered to obey, granted fortitude to faithfully wait for His return amidst this world filled with tribulations. This is the answer to our discontentment in life; He makes our hearts content as we rest in Him. Not that we no longer recognize that our situations are less than perfect but we no longer view our circumstances as ultimate, we no longer use them as an excuse to give in, to run away, to quit fighting the fight of faith, to despair.

This renewal grants us a new heart, and new affections. Our affections are set free from lies, from idols, from insecurities. The tribulations we walk through can cloud our thinking, whether it be pain, loss, abandonment, sickness. Turning to God, abiding in His Word and looking to Him for renewal undoes the damage of these tribulations. We can finally believe that He is all we need, that He does fulfill our longings, that He will never leave us. We can finally live out of God's love, enjoying a 'faith working through love' (see Gal. 5:5-6). God's love, rather than lesser loves, will constrain us.

Sometimes we need renewal, but the feelings and thoughts we have in these times are misleading, and instead of seeking renewal we run away, or think we simply need 'me time.' 1 Timothy 6:12 would direct us otherwise, commanding us to fight! Fight for joy and satisfaction and eternal life that is only found in Jesus. We do not need a break from it all, we need to get deeper into our life in Christ. We ought not try to merely run away from our lot in life. Instead we find a secluded place, in order to seek His grace in the midst of the storm, we seek our true refuge. Time seeking the Lord, resting in Him, digging deeper into the wellspring of life will have us fighting rather than giving in. It will have us laying down the contrary thoughts and feelings at the cross and picking up truth and joy and peace. As you gaze upon and think upon God's goodness and truth and beauty and majesty, He will guard your hearts and minds from the *zeitgeist* of 'just do you' so you can be enraptured in true love and glory. Sometimes we need the help of friends with the same attitude of Paul, friends who are truly 'workers with [us] for [our] joy' (see 2 Cor. 1:24). God the Son came in the flesh that we might have joy. True fellowship will seek God's joy with and for one another.

Filled with His Fullness

One important truth that Paul knew the Colossians needed to bask in was that of being filled. This was first discussed in chapter five, but here we relate His fullness to our soul's craving for true glory. In understanding this, we cease seeking our identity or satisfaction in other sources which detract from our delighting in the simplicity of devotion to Christ. The fountainhead fills us, and as the Gospel of John states plainly, 'of His fullness we have all received' (John 1:16). His fullness is never depleted, never trickles, never lessens, never runs out. He has rivers of living water to offer, not small sippy cups. Christ's fullness is such an important concept, that one of the most beautiful prayers offered up for the Ephesians ends this way:

> For this reason I bow my knees before the Father, from whom every family in heaven and on earth derives its name, that He would grant you, according to the riches of His glory, to be strengthened with power through His Spirit in the inner man, so that Christ may dwell in your hearts through faith; and that you, being rooted and grounded in love, may be able to comprehend with all the saints what is the breadth and length and height and depth, and to know the love of Christ which surpasses knowledge, that you may be filled up to all the fullness of God (Eph. 3:14-19).

Because we have received of His fullness, we can find in Christ enough supply to be steadfast, to endure, and to overcome. We all receive our name from Him, He is the head of the family we are adopted into, we are God's household, we belong. Rest in that beloved, and delight in that; such a mindset will renew you. How rich are the 'riches of His glory'? Will you exhaust them? Spend some time meditating on that, along with Ephesians 1:7-8, 2:4-7, and 3:8. The creator's riches can never fully be fathomed. Next, in verse 17 of the passage quoted above, we are asked to imagine ourselves as 'rooted and grounded in love,' so not only are we a branch connected to the vine, we understand that the roots are planted deep in the love of God. We find renewal by being planted by God, receiving of His sap, and drinking deeply through roots embedded in His love. We are a tree planted by streams of living water, delighting to meditate on God's Word day and night, fruitful and full of life no matter the season (Psalm 1). All this, by His filling. He fills us with His love, and true knowledge, which He then employs to renew and strengthen our inner being. As we are filled with His fullness, our desire for earthly validation fades, we find that His love and His opinion of us really do outweigh all the lesser glory we could seek from family, friends, or neighbors. God's love has no substitutes. Abide in His love.

Overcoming

Through faith, which is born of God, a gift of God, and is authored by God, we overcome one of the greatest enemies to our soul – this fallen world. As we find ourselves clinging to God's Word, manifesting His truth, growing as we put off the old and put on the new, renewed in our inner person, we will also find ourselves pitted in battle against the world. Not creation per se, but all that once honored God in the garden, but now loves darkness, destruction, decay, deceitfulness, and blasphemy. The world comes at us mostly as ideas, shouted in our direction, emblazoned on billboards, and smoothly slipping into our minds as we delight in a little entertainment, be it book, movie, video game, social media, or careless conversation. Consider for a moment how John pastored his congregation to be aware of the world, and their relation to it:

> ... the Christ is born of God, and whoever loves the Father loves the child born of Him ... For this is the love of God, that we keep His commandments; and His commandments are not burdensome. For whatever is born of God overcomes the world; and this is the victory that overcomes the world—our faith. Who is the one who overcomes the world, but he who believes that Jesus is the Son of God? (1 John 5:1, 3-5).

Our faith overcomes the world? Yes, the battle rages, and our days on earth are spent overcoming as we walk by faith. The world does not have the last word, the world does not define us, or define reality. The world cannot separate us from the love of God though it ensnares us for a moment. The world is subject to future judgment, but we do not fear that judgment, we remember Christ has drunk the cup of God's wrath for us. Rather we go boldly before our God and find mercy every time. Mercy, and strength, and help. By faith we walk in His ancient paths and overcome every contrary idea thrown at us, every label and pigeonhole.

We overcome by faith, because '... the world has been crucified to me, and I to the world' (Gal. 6:14). The world hates children of God, and when we stop trying to live in the world as though it were our only home, we feel the sting of that hatred. It is okay to grieve this, to cry out to the Lord that this is hard. We live in a world that is not truly our home. We can never make it a perfect place, and we must somehow seek understanding from Him on how to crucify the world to ourselves. But we move on from grieving the world's hatred by basking in His great love, shown on the cross. The world is crucified to you when your highest glory and delight are not found therein. Christ is our life and has given us a far greater possession than any we see here; set your hearts' affections on Him, work for the treasure that does not rot or decay. Crucify your desire to please the world around you and seek to have thoughts and actions pleasing to the one who created, redeemed, and sustains you. Grace will reign! (See Rom. 5:19-21).

As discussed earlier, pondering of our hope is crucial for our hearts and souls, it is a very necessary part of abiding in Him. In the Epistles to the seven churches in Revelation, each Epistle ends with a promise of hope to overcomers.

In these Epistles, overcoming is carried out by means of keeping His words, keeping His deeds, being zealous, repenting, and partaking of the perseverance found in Him (see 1:9–3:22). The promises are all ones fulfilled in heaven; we await them eagerly. Meditating on them will help you see how these fulfill so many longings that we try to satisfy with earthly things. Overcoming includes setting our affections on these heavenly promises rather than on earthly means of satisfaction. Our ultimate satisfaction awaits, and we cling to the hope of that. We long, and instead of settling for worldly satisfaction we crucify the world's empty offers and run after Christ's offers. He holds out to us the crown of life, plenteous fruit from the tree of life, hidden manna, a new name (oh study this sometime beloved, the white stone mentioned in Revelation 2:12-17 symbolizes such a beautiful concept), shared authority from Him, walking with Him, hearing our name confessed by Jesus in front of the Father, being clothed with pure beauty, a purpose and delightful duty in the house of God, and sitting with Jesus on His throne. There is much symbolized here, much that fulfills every longing that may arise in you. Start with the promise of 'walking with Him'. Let yourself spend some time meditating on what that could be like. Imagine sharing your favorite moments in His presence, with a purified heart fully capable of taking in all the joy He offers. Meditate slowly enough to memorize these promises, cling to them.

His renewal makes us more fully human, more alive, more of who we were created to be, and full of the perseverance necessary to wait eagerly for Him to complete the work begun in you. When we seek the rest (Jer. 6:16) that we all desperately long for from God alone, we will experience it and will be changed by it.

Practices

Take a prayer and worship walk (or hike, if you like), and start putting this on your calendar more regularly. As you walk, recite Scripture, pray; and marvel at His works. Be in His creation to see, hear, smell, and be in awe of Him. Creation will reveal to us a bit about His nature, and His invisible attributes. Only Scripture reveals Christ as our Redeemer, but His works are still wonderful to behold, and can refresh and teach us.

Spend time picturing familiar Gospel stories. Picture the compassion Jesus has for His own. Picture Jesus looking at you with that compassion. How will times like this renew your view of yourself, and let the reality of His compassion sink in to renew your affections?

Muse upon Isaiah 26:3, and the life and peace promised in Romans 8. Faith is believing God will do what He promises, so look to Him for this life and peace; it is not a far-fetched dream. Do not mistake an easy life, or good feelings for that which is truly promised.

Spend one moment pondering your chains, and Jeremiah 17, and an hour at least pondering Jeremiah 31:1-3, 25, 33-34. Write down verses that remind you of who God says you are in Christ, and the unchangeableness of His ways.

Read through the first four chapters in Revelation, trusting that the ones who read and hear these words, truly hearing and taking them to heart, are blessed. Find all the promises made to 'overcomers' and journal through those verses. Keep these promises, pray through these chapters, and cling to the 'Living One' who is standing at the door knocking.

Start the habit of weekly preparing for the Sabbath, which was made for man. How can you rest if you convince yourself you have to do this work? On Saturday, prepare like you would for a vacation. Clean extra, prepare extra food, etc. Usher the day of rest in by actively engaging your mind ahead of time. Confess your need for rest, what you most want Him to work in you, ways you need refreshing. Pray expectantly, that He would meet these soul needs. Let your last thoughts Saturday night be from God's Word rather than social media, contrary movies or highly opinionated news. Set your mind especially on the eve of the day set aside for worship, and you will find rest and renewal. Having renewed minds ushers us into the unity of the Spirit reserved for the true church (Eph. 4:3, Rom. 8). Find some books that will become familiar friends. On any given Sabbath, spend time with your old friend, re-reading passages that feed your soul, draw you to worship, and call you away from the desire to solve worldly concerns. (Tozer, Packer, Owen, Edwards, Calvin, Bonhoeffer, Stott, Lewis, and Athenasius are some of my old friends.)

8

Always Becoming

There is a daily-ness to the life we are called to. There is much in this life that we must attend to daily without growing weary. This begins when we die daily, for in our own flesh we cannot walk. He will fill us, so that we may walk in a manner that suits one of His kingdom subjects (see Col. 3). On this side of heaven we never fully attain the life He has called us to, or the glory, or the perfection. We will ever be fighting an inner battle against sin, depending on God, learning from Him, growing in Christlikeness, and walking in the command to grow in grace and knowledge. In God's mercy, He patiently and gradually reveals more and more of our own flesh to us, that we may run to His cross anew. Even in this we do not grow weary, but rejoice in how great God's salvation is, and how mercifully kind He remains. We are all born persons, born in the image of God though tarnished by sin. After becoming a child of God we must all admit we are not yet whole or perfect. He will complete that work when He takes us home; meanwhile in union with Christ we are always becoming our real self.

John 1 tells us that we have received of 'His fullness' (see John 1:14-16). We do not receive apart from God, as though

He handed us something and left us alone. God calls us to life in Himself. He is our eternal source of life, and we are ever becoming more like Him, more alive. Paul explained to the Galatian church that his burden for them was that Christ would take shape in each of them (Gal. 4:19). Not that they would be found perfect apart from Christ, but that they would be united to Him and while still sojourning here on earth, become like Him. We find our life in Him, but do not then go our own way, we cry out that it is no longer I who live, but Christ in me. We sigh with contentment that we are not caught up in futility, but have purpose, a hope, and constant access to our sustainer. We abide.

Dynamic, Not Static

The nature of the Christian life is to grow, to become more fully who we are in Christ, to be further conformed to the image of Christ. He awakens us to this new life, active and flowing and flourishing, not at all static and stale. There is always more to know. We cannot fathom the depth of His being, but by His Spirit we will grow deeper in the knowledge of Him as we daily seek, cling, and otherwise abide and rest in Him. Settling for the pure milk of the Word, which was so satisfying in your early years as a Christian, will leave you feeling unsatisfied and wilting in your whole being; milk will not foster the growth intended. Contrarily, the abiding life will be fruitful, despite earthly limitations, and flourishing inwardly as spring blossoms respond to the spring rains and sunshine. We can be led into the steadfastness of Christ, finding strength for the journey. We can persevere in His strength and fortitude. And we journey on, further into the life He has for us, pressing on.

The daily-ness we are all called to is not a five minute devotion of thought, or merely a morning prayer and evening prayer. It is a constant connection, a continual growth, a dependence in and through every moment. It is living in light of Romans 11:36, acknowledging that 'from Him and through Him and to Him are all things.' The life He has called us to is not a checklist to complete, it can never be completed, it is the beginning of our eternal life. We are now to take hold of the eternal life, which has a quality vaster than we can imagine, but only one source. It is sometimes the quantity that causes us to set our minds on other things, how can one really grasp the forever-ness? But if we set our minds instead on the quality of eternal life, the characteristics of that life, then our hearts will be drawn to ponder it more, and we will boast in Him all the more.

2 Peter 1 is a beautiful passage to muse upon when considering this 'always becoming' nature of our Christian life:

> To those who have received a faith of the same kind as ours, by the righteousness of our God and Savior, Jesus Christ: Grace and peace be multiplied to you in the knowledge of God and of Jesus our Lord; seeing that His divine power has granted to us everything pertaining to life and godliness, through the true knowledge of Him who called us by His own glory and excellence. For by these He has granted to us His precious and magnificent promises, so that by them you may become partakers of *the* divine nature, having escaped the corruption that is in the world by lust. Now for this very reason also, applying all diligence, in your faith supply moral excellence, and in *your* moral excellence, knowledge, and in *your* knowledge, self-control, and in *your* self-control, perseverance, and in *your* perseverance, godliness, and in *your* godliness, brotherly kindness, and in *your* brotherly kindness, love. For if these *qualities* are yours and are increasing, they render you neither useless nor unfruitful in the true knowledge of our Lord Jesus Christ (2 Pet. 1:1-8).

We have received faith but notice the relation of knowledge to the growth that follows. Notice all that is multiplied to us as we seek Him. Notice how this list overlaps with what we know to be fruits of the Spirit from Galatians 5 (which is not an exhaustive list). The Spirit calls us to faithful, daily obedience. And He grows us, making us more like Christ as we respond with active obedience. To abide in Him is to take heed, to obey, to pay attention to His Word. The Spirit works it into our hearts, and we become more like the Word we are delighting in.

The promise of this passage is that we will be fruitful in the knowledge of Christ, the knowledge that we can never reach the end of. The personal knowledge He gives will take root in your heart, and will be made manifest in your obedience, as you not only accept but act upon the Word implanted (see James 1:21-25), being a faithful keeper of God's Word. We can never grow bored or weary, as He will ever be revealing more of His infinite self to our finite selves. The Spirit carries this out through what many theologians call 'illumination' or the illumining of our minds (briefly defined in the introduction). He grants us to know, He opens our eyes further and deeper. We gaze, He illumines. We are now looking into a mirror dimly, but we do not grow discouraged and look away for that reason. We continue to gaze because He promised to manifest Himself further to His own. Imagine for a moment that you were one of those disciples on the road to Emmaus. Jesus walks up and continues the journey with you, and explains how the Christ came to fulfill all that was written in the Law, the Prophets, and other Old Testament writings. Would that not be amazing, and would your heart soar as theirs did? Now think upon Jesus telling His twelve disciples during the last supper that the Father would send the Spirit of truth, and that it would be better for Him to leave. The Spirit's ministry to the church in this regard is to open up for us the meaning of all that God spoke, all the Scriptures that are God-breathed, so that we too may understand. This is the anointing spoken of in 1 John.

Waiting

Galatians 5 reminds us that we who are living by faith are '… waiting for the hope of righteousness' (Gal. 5:5). Perhaps the most frustrating part of our always becoming, never fully arriving at perfection here, is that so much of it is waiting. We turn to Christ, He works, but we must wait for the completion of His work in us. And in waiting, He makes us patient and humble, like Himself. Some of this waiting is passive, being still, resisting the urge for more striving. Yet sometimes our waiting feels more like Paul describes in Philippians, 'pressing on, reaching' or as he instructed Timothy, to take hold of the eternal life to which he was called (1 Tim. 6:12). If our waiting has this hope in view, the peace that God promises washes away our frustrations. The hope of righteousness, with a home in the land where righteousness reigns, helps us whether we are resting or pressing on. Now, in union with Christ we can say to ourselves:

> But by His doing you are in Christ Jesus, who became to us wisdom from God, and righteousness and sanctification, and redemption, so that, just as it is written, 'LET HIM WHO BOASTS, BOAST IN THE LORD' (1 Cor. 1:30-31).

He is all this for me, my life is hid in Him, so I will wait patiently and expectantly for my hope of righteousness.

Concerning the obedience we are called to, keep in mind it is not the law that makes us righteous, holy, pure, blameless, knowledgeable, or full of joy and peace. It is Christ alone, to whom the law points (spend some time in Galatians 3:1–4:7).

No one has kept God's commands perfectly, so what further could we prescribe to please Him? We need only pursue the righteousness that comes through faith. In place of self-effort and self-righteousness is gazing at and adoring our perfect mediator, Christ. We look to the cross, to the resurrection, to the mediator who sits on His throne, and we look nowhere else. Our mediator, gloriously and perfectly God, took on flesh and dwelt among us. He takes our sin, gives us His own righteousness, and in His humility has reconciled us to God. As we look to Jesus in all this, we see perfect love, and power. And we become our true selves. We do not fear losing our old self, when once we truly see His glory with eyes of faith.

He alone will make us whole, heal us, and recreate us in the true image. And then, walking by faith, in His light, can we please Him who fulfilled the law on our behalf. We can walk in faith and repentance, rather than in disappointment at our inability to perfectly carry out the law.

Yet, even Paul spoke often of the 'obedience of faith' and so Jesus taught of our fruitfulness as we abide in Him (see Romans 1:5 and 16:25-27). Our righteousness is by faith, not by works of the law. Once we begin this journey, we are given new desires, new strength, new life, and thereby the possibility of true obedience. In heart, mind, soul and body we can follow Him, and as His life takes root we become more like Him. Ever becoming more obedient. Paul was delighted to see the progress of faith in those he had preached the gospel to, '…resulting in the obedience of the Gentiles by word and deed' (Rom. 15:18). John was delighted to see his followers walking in truth and love (see 2 John and 3 John). This should ever be increasing in us as we live out our days here on earth. God will ever be pruning, and we become ever more fruitful. In looking to Father, Son and Spirit, we find all our hearts' desire for purpose and belonging fulfilled.

Divine Nature

Abiding in Christ, we also find the excellencies our imaginations crave to feast upon. We all ought to be theologians, really. Theology is not for elders and professionals only. We were all created and brought into this fellowship to magnify Him, to declare His excellencies, to share the divine nature. What is theology? The queen of all sciences, the study of God who created everything by speaking, of God who speaks that we may know Him. A theologian is one who seeks after this knowledge of God as God has revealed Himself, who is willing to glorify Him, adore Him, and to seek to know Him more deeply. Being a theologian means believing that eternal life is knowing Him and desiring to be known by God above earthly treasures. Contemplate John 17:3. We find great satisfaction from any relationship in which we feel known, yet any such experience is only a foretaste of what God wants us to experience with Him (see also Gal. 4:9). Cry out to Him, that He would lead you into the simplicity and purity of devotion to Christ, into worshiping in truth. As He teaches you in His Word, let that knowledge shape your hopes, dreams, expectations, reactions, worldview, conversations, and time management. You are not your own, you are not the star of your own story, you are not an island, you are so much more. Your story is part of God's story. You were called into His family, into the kingdom of priests, into the church of the living God, into fellowship with the Trinity and with all others who know Him.

All that comprises His divine nature is glory, true glory. God's divine attributes can be seen throughout His creation, the heavens truly do declare His glory. Yet, His glory, His divine nature is most clearly seen in the incarnation. It was the Father's good pleasure to carry out redemption in this way alone. We are further conformed to God's image as we gaze upon Jesus who came to be seen. He came to reveal what had been hidden from all past generations, and still remains hidden to those who do not know Him. But to us who are united to Christ, who have been given eyes to see and know Him, to us He gives us a fuller glimpse, though it is still dim on this side of heaven.

When Peter is helping the churches scattered abroad understand our calling to partake of the divine nature, he lists out the things we ought to add and work on. Looking at what Peter taught, we know that in union with Christ, Jesus becomes to us '… wisdom, righteousness, sanctification and redemption' (1 Cor. 1:30). But He also pours into us love, joy, peace, patience, and all the other fruits of the Spirit. Faith, kindness, knowledge, and so many more. To be these is to be like Him. These are His qualities, we grow in them only as we grow in our intimate, familial knowledge of Him as He has revealed Himself.

Identity and Purpose

Perhaps the easiest way to be led astray from the simplicity and purity of devotion to Christ is forgetting that our identity is complete in Him. We think we know ourselves, our true selves. The world tells us we ought to be in the process of making ourselves. We don't admit it, but sometimes we act as though we were the center of the universe. We come to Christ and ask that He accept us and keep us as is, or expect that He bless our desires however contrary to His glory they are. Some fear the difference they will discover as they put on the new self.

If we continually exchange God's glory for a lesser one, no wonder we are so discontented with life. Let His words define you, and shape you, as you discover in them meaning and purpose and eternal life. We have the great privilege of seeing and knowing His glory and doing everything unto Him. As we do, we become more of who He has created us to be, and more joyful and contented with the life He has called us to. When I first started reading John Owen's works, I noticed how often he used the word 'complacency' in a positive manner. Most of my life I had heard the word 'complacent' used of people full of pride and smugness and lack of desire to keep moving forward. A complacent person is currently thought to be one unmoved by a situation, lazy, careless, unmotivated or even void of passion. Reading John Owen challenged me, I needed to find the older definition of this word. It was then that I discovered that, as is often the case, Americans recently redefined this word. A complacent person used to be marked by having found their true passion, and was one who rested contentedly in it, not lazily, but not easily swayed to a lesser passion. A person who complacently abides in Christ is one who has found in Him the source of all that is good, true, beautiful and glorious. Oh that we would complacently rest in Him, finding satisfaction in Christ alone, and trusting Christ to be our ultimate good!

As His words define you, and shape you, you will be enabled to do all things unto Him. He is steadfast and unchanging. This fallen world is filled with idols that deteriorate, and otherwise change. Jobs change, addresses change, friends move, friends grow distant, the culture around is in constant flux, seasons come and go. Yet God does not change, and who He says you are will not change with the world. Who you are becomes more clear to you as you gaze at Him rather than at the world. Your old self being crucified makes room for the new, and you discover the real you that God has known and loved, the person He has made you to be. It takes great self-discipline to let go of worldly identities, and to align your thinking with His, but it is not impossible. And it brings great relief to know that 'who I am' is not something foisted upon me by the world, nor something I can somehow mess up or lose. Dying to self brings about the true self, so with great joy and complacency we dig deep into Christ, looking for the longings of our souls to be satisfied.

Prayers of the Abiding Ones

Becoming more like Christ, more of your true self, will impact how you relate to your God. Your prayer life will always be becoming purer, more intimate, more pleasing to Him and you. So much doubt and despair fills the hearts of those who continuously wonder whether they are praying right or need more faith. Perhaps we should ask a different question, 'Jesus, teach me to pray!' Spending a season in the gospel accounts, looking for all that He taught, must also take into account that we should not turn any one verse on prayer into a new law. Studying these Scriptures together gives a broad picture, a beautiful tapestry. He taught us to persevere in prayer, to not lose heart, to continue and press on. He taught us the importance of having 'Thy will be done' undergird all that we pour out of our hearts. He taught that God loves to give His Spirit, even though we selfishly ask for mere materialism and frown upon the power and peace available in the Spirit. Jesus taught in John 15:7, that if we are abiding in Him, and His words are abiding in us, then we will have what we ask for. What would you be asking for if you truly spent most of your waking hours meditating on His Word, delighting in His Word, and less time in other words? What if all your spare moments, and the time completing habitual tasks, found you musing upon Scripture? Scripture would direct your prayers, and what you ask for and how you ask for it would change. God's Word will be active in us, refining us and this will be evidenced in our prayers. He draws us into this relationship and loves the interchange and will be giving us hearts and lips with which to glorify Him and join Him in His work. He works through our prayers, but not because we are clever, or independently wise. When His words are abiding in us, our prayers will not be a list of things we want. Yet we will pour out our hearts, ask for help and wisdom and everything we need. And with His presence He will answer, with His peace He will guard us (see Phil. 4:4-9), and assuredly He will act (see Isa. 64:4; Psalm 138:8).

Enjoying Him now, delighting in Him now, increasing now, is all part of this relationship in which He is making us new and bringing His work toward completion. Not enjoying these now should cause us to pause, to question. If I cannot give more than five minutes thought to God in a day, why? What is holding me back? What idol have I set before me? If these qualities Peter mentions (see quote above) are mine and ever increasing, if I am ever becoming more like Jesus then I am reassured of His work in me. If this work is not happening, what am I assured of? Am I really gazing at Christ and abiding in Him? Do I desire the pure milk of the Word, and am I moving on to desire the steak, oven roasted vegetables, fresh baked bread and butter, with a glass of sweet red wine? Seek, and you will find. Knock and it will be opened. Ask God for the insatiable desire to grow and know Him, and He will give it, He loves to give His Spirit, and pour His love into our hearts!

We will never plumb the depths of His love, His grace, and all that He longs to pour into us. His thoughts do not have to grow boring or mundane, as though familiarity with an infinitely glorious God could breed contempt. Rather, the Spirit who is an ever-flowing stream of living water, will be pouring His freshness into us. Romans 11:30–12:2 encourages us in this, His Word is ever fresh and full.

But now you have been shown mercy! ... Oh the depth of the riches both of the wisdom and knowledge of God! How unsearchable are His judgments and unfathomable His ways! ... for from Him and through Him and to Him are all things. To Him be the glory forever ... (Rom. 11:30, 33, 36).

He has called us into His glory, and while we are yet in this world He is ever fitting us for it.

Practices

Journal through Psalm 19, focus on verses about His worth, more than gold, sweeter than honey. Is He that to you? Is He your treasure, as you are His? Does He restore your soul? You become what you treasure, you will grow to be like Him when He is your greatest love.

Read through Colossians 1:1–2:5. Colossians was a letter written as encouragement in the face of difficulty in life, to a city experiencing decline, with the rise of false teaching surrounding the church. There was a lot of 'Christ and' asceticism, legalism, law keeping, appeasing other powers and authorities, or discovering supposedly secret knowledge. What sort of 'Christ and _____' do you need to lay down? As you lay these down, be encouraged to pray for yourself the prayer offered for the Colossians:

- to be filled with knowledge that God reveals in His Word
- to gain spiritual wisdom and understanding, a gift from the Spirit not from my effort
- to experience walking in a manner pleasing to the Lord as the fruit of faith
- to trust that this filling and gaining and walking shall ultimately lead to a fruitful life and increased intimate knowledge of God, and the attaining of steadfastness and patience
- To resist the temptation to put the cart before the horse

(i.e. walk in this manner, believing that then suddenly you'll love and know God deeply)

Meditate on how this passage, a song from the early age of the church, is meant to dispel doubts and false teachings and fears in the hearts of those who know Him. This passage displays Christ as being above all, supreme, victorious. Surely it will enlarge our hearts as we read and re-read.

Journal through the roles you play in life, list them out: child of God, spouse, parent, sibling, Bible Study teacher, friend, neighbor. Then spend some time writing out a few Scriptures to pray through for each role. Remind yourself to come back to these prayers occasionally, that you would recognize God's work in you as you become more like Him.

9

Partaker

_____

We who are in union with Christ are said to be partakers of His nature, His glory, His sufferings, His perseverance, and are to be co-heirs. If we are honest, there are times when we don't want to share in God's glory, we want our own. We exchange the free offer of streams of living water for broken cisterns. But as we become 'partakers of the divine nature' our enjoyment of and desire for His glory above our own grows.

> Seeing that His divine power has granted to us everything pertaining to life and godliness, through the true knowledge of Him who called us by His own glory and excellence. For by these He has granted to us His precious and magnificent promises, so that by them you may become partakers of the divine nature, having escaped the corruption that is in the world by lust (2 Pet. 1:3-4).

Though we are partakers we are never equal. As partakers in the divine nature, our natures are no longer slaves to corruption, He is undoing the curse we had been subject to. In our true knowledge of Him we behold His glory dimly now, with the hope of seeing Him clearly and face to face. But

He is transforming us as we abide in Him, and to Him alone is all the praise and honor! As partakers of His divine nature we are to the praise of His glory and grace (see Eph. 1:6, 12).

Because we are sensual creatures, He came, and our senses behold. After His people denied His witness in creation and through the prophets, He came. In the fullness of times, He came. And we know truth and love by His coming. The Word dwelt among us, revealing everlasting truth in words and deeds; He made God known. Yet it was not plain for all to 'see,' only those who walk by faith saw the glimpses of His glory (John 10:23-26). For now, we trust what has been revealed, anticipating a time when we see Him face to face. Before Jesus came there were only shadows and glimpses. Now through the true image, He is revealed and the mystery laid bare for us. He revealed all this in word and deed. Be careful lest you believe one is important and the other disposable.

We can seek to know, gaze truly, and partake. As partakers of the divine nature, we are in the practice of putting off the old self corrupted by lust, and putting on the new self. To spend some time meditating on this, read through Ephesians 4 and Colossians 2–3. While considering what you've put off, remember that Christ came to partake of flesh and blood, yet without giving in to the temptations that we succumb to (see Heb. 2). Our flesh is weak and can never produce the righteousness God requires. Jesus partook of flesh without ceasing to be fully God, and in this act He calls us brethren. He humbled Himself to partake of flesh with this in view: our own partaking in His divine nature.

Fellowship
Here and now, as we abide in Him, we partake in the fellowship He longed to draw us into. (See 1 John 1:1-3; and

John 17). This mystical communion is no program, there is no 'how to' because this is nothing that flesh and blood can produce. 'It is the Spirit who gives life' (John 6:63) and we receive it, we take hold of it. In this fellowship we can know and experience all the love and belonging we desire – we find our Father, Brother, Lover, Friend. We are continually assured of God's love for us, and of our belonging to Him, with Him, in His kingdom.

We also partake in the sufferings, with the hope of heaven in mind:

> The Spirit Himself testifies with our spirit that we are children of God, and if children, heirs also, heirs of God and fellow heirs with Christ, if indeed we suffer with *Him* so that we may also be glorified with *Him* (Rom. 8:16-17).

In Christ, part of our kingdom responsibility is to carry 'about in the body the dying of Jesus, so that the life of Jesus also may be manifested in our body' (2 Cor. 4:10). We know Him in His sufferings, we ponder His cross, we pick up our cross and follow Him. In this partaking, we realize that none of our earthly trials are ultimate. They will not last forever, nor determine my eternal outcome. They do not define me now, nor mar God's love and affections toward me, nor change His purposes for my life. Rather, Christ's life becomes visible through us who partake in His sufferings. It becomes visible because we are inwardly renewed (we are weak, He is strong). He is holding us and keeping us, filling us with His strength.

> But to the degree that you share the sufferings of Christ, keep on rejoicing, so that also at the revelation of His glory you may rejoice with exultation (1 Pet. 4:13).

We do not rejoice because suffering does not hurt, our rejoicing is deeper. On the contrary, our whole being actually suffers. Knowing the '… fellowship of His suffering …' is necessarily prior to our experience of perfection and glory (see Phil. 3:10). Yet, in the suffering, we rejoice in His nearness, His power, His majesty, and His extravagant grace. We rejoice knowing our eternal redemption is drawing ever nearer. We must be careful not to compare our experience of suffering with others. The plans God has for each of us are unique, yet we all share in His sufferings. Whether physical pain or illness, or grief and loss, or loneliness, or betrayal, or weariness, or emotional angst and pain, abuse at the hand of others, or limitations that hold us back. No suffering is more or less a sharing in Christ's suffering. As we sojourn here, we suffer. But we also hope, knowing the 'weight of glory' this suffering leads to (see 2 Cor. 4:17). God will create in us hearts full of goodness, capable of enjoying pure love and beauty and glory. We partake and endure and exult trusting our redeemer in this process.

Suffering, Perseverance

We know that reading or hearing the book of Revelation brings great encouragement, as chapter one states. While first addressing his audience, John calls himself '… your brother and fellow partaker of tribulation and kingdom and perseverance *which are* in Jesus …' (Rev. 1:9). As we abide in Him, we too partake in tribulation (which we've already touched on) but also perseverance, endurance, fortitude to not only survive these times but also overcome. Have you noticed the number of times John uses the word 'overcome' in the letters to the seven churches? Connect this with his encouragement in 1 John that we are those who overcome by faith. We are fellow partakers, are we not? As we partake of sufferings and tribulation, we can think of the countless hostilities Jesus faced, but also the broken relationships (ponder just how often his brothers sneered and mocked), the attacks of the evil one, and the general malaise of people He had come to rescue. All of this, we will face this. We are not called to a garden of sunshine and roses; we look eagerly to our heavenly home while enduring the tribulations of this world. His perseverance and His strength are ours too.

As partakers in Jesus' kingdom, we live each moment in light of His teaching that the kingdom was at hand with His incarnation. Jesus brought that kingdom with Him, ushers us into it, and now we are that kingdom of priests. We must heed the lessons from His sermon on the mount, and take to heart the teachings found here in Revelation, in 1 Peter, in Romans and elsewhere, that we partake of this kingdom now. We set up Christ as Lord and King in our hearts, presenting ourselves to Him as subjects. Beloved subjects; fully loved and welcomed. As we abide in the presence of our King we are enabled to manifest Christ as the Light, the Way, the Truth, and the Love that all mankind are searching for. We are weak, but we look to Him who is our strength; and march forward to the beat of His drum. We do not panic and try to speed up Christ's work. He is patient, steadfast, and will succeed in all His purposes. The Prince of Peace bore our sins, partook of our reproaches and the wrath due to us, that we might persevere, endure, and even overcome.

Glory

Peter calls those in ministry among the dispersed believers in Asia partakers 'also of the glory that is to be revealed' and speaks of the crown of glory offered to all who follow Jesus (1 Pet. 5:1,4). He closes the letter with this call and promise:

> ... [Stand] firm in your faith, knowing that the same experiences of suffering are being accomplished by your brethren who are in the world. After you have suffered for a

little while, the God of all grace, who called you to His eternal glory in Christ, will Himself perfect, confirm, strengthen *and* establish you (1 Pet. 5:9-10).

What strength we find when we ponder the crown of glory that awaits! What fortitude we experience when we trust the promises of our heavenly home. We partake of sufferings now, but of glory then. Paul too focuses on future glory telling the Colossians that 'When Christ, who is our life, is revealed, then you too will be revealed …' (Col. 3:4). Life was difficult in Colossea during this time, economic hardships and religious persecutions abounded. Yet, they were to focus their gaze heavenward, think of their future with Christ, who would return, and therein find strength and perseverance. Partaking now of His sufferings, while thinking about the future partaking of His glory.

The Power of God

Paul's message to the Corinthians begins with a retelling of what God has done in them, that they were '… enriched in Him, in all speech and all knowledge.' (1 Cor. 1:5). He then makes two very bold statements we would do well to cling to, concerning the power of God in the lives of believers.

> For the word of the cross is foolishness to those who are perishing, but to us who are being saved it is the power of God. … we preach Christ crucified, to Jews a stumbling block and to Gentiles foolishness, but to those who are the called, both Jews and Greeks, Christ the power of God and the wisdom of God (1 Cor. 1:18, 23-24).

The one true God speaks, and His Word is power. Power to bring us to life, to overcome temptation and tribulation, to heal and make new, to refresh the soul that languishes and to grow us continually. We do not rightly partake of fellowship with Him without coming to hear His Word. We do not continue steadfastly if we lay aside all that He has revealed and look elsewhere, or sulk hopelessly as though His Word was void of power. Our faith is in the '… power of God' and not in the cleverness of preachers, or wittiness of devotional writers (see 1 Cor. 2:5). As promised by Jesus, the helper has come. The Spirit dwells in us who are truly His. And this Spirit that we have received enables us to '…know the things freely given to us by God, which things we also speak, not in words taught by human wisdom, but in those taught by the Spirit …' (1 Cor. 2:12-13). Ultimately, we belong to God and have all that we need (1 Cor. 3:22-23).

Partakers of Christ

He called His disciples to partake of the bread of life, and then asked them to believe that Jesus is that very bread. Eat of His flesh? Yes, figuratively. John 6:33-69 details the conversation revealing Himself as the bread come down out of heaven. He speaks of the beginning of faith, the first bite if you will. If you receive His death on the cross as your redemption, then you have eaten His flesh and you do abide with Him. If you look for more, or other ways of finding God you are doomed. No other miracle, not the manna in the wilderness or the loaves and fishes on the hillside, which displays God's glory, will ever give you eternal life. Jesus alone gives this life; it is His joy to do it. We cannot come to Him for the beginning, and go astray finding our own path, finding new words, finding different means of grace. 'For we have become partakers of Christ, if we hold fast the beginning of our assurance firm until the end' (Heb. 3:14). This 'if' is not designed to bring doubt, but assurance. If we come to Him, He gives us eternal life. It is eternal, the quality of this life can never be marred, never wane. This life will never cease, be destroyed, or corrupted. This life has purpose and joy, it is grasped by faith here and by sight in heaven. We who receive it will hold fast to it.

The 'if' serves to remind us of the greatness of the salvation, the extent, the eternality. And so we resolve to hold fast to the one who upholds all things by His powerful Word, and who holds His own in His grip such that none can snatch us out.

Practices

Read through 2 Peter 1 once more; set aside time for study of this passage. Journal through what the 'precious and magnificent promises' are. Write them down, rephrase them, pray through them, write about your experience of or desire for them.

Journal through the character qualities that are the new self we are to put on, compare Ephesians 4 and Colossians 2–3. List out what you see, turn this into something you can pray through. Then turn to Romans 13:11-14; read slowly and focus on the main verbs and nouns and the imagery used. Picture yourself 'putting on the Lord Jesus Christ' and slowly meditate on this process.

Spend time each day for a season (perhaps a week, a month, etc.) praying through Psalm 105:1-5; and 2 Thessalonians 1:11-12. Pray this for yourself, that you would seek Him continuously, that His glory would be evident in your life. Journal through how praying these Scriptures may have enlarged your heart or otherwise grown you.

Read through Ephesians 1:1-14 and Ephesians 3:6-8; journal through these verses meditating on His lavish grace, His kind intentions, His glory, the mystery revealed, the promises made, and the unfathomable riches of Christ.

Contemplate 2 Timothy 4:7-8. Have you loved His appearing? Does His incarnation warm your heart, calm your fears, speak to your struggles? Take some time to do so. Find other Scripture references (perhaps starting in Matthew 5–6, and 19, Luke 12 and 14), and journal through these verses. Can your heavenly reward motivate you daily?

10

Abiding in Truth and Love

John, the apostle who also authored a Gospel account, three Epistles and Revelation, was also one of the inner three (Peter, James and John) who went with Jesus alone at times (witnessing miracles, praying). He is responsible for acts of healing according to Acts 3–4, but most notably is known as the disciple whom Jesus loved. Jesus' love is not exclusive, this was not the claim John was making. Rather, he is displaying his own great trust in the fullness of Jesus' love. John was also concerned for the truth. Love and truth are inseparable in scriptural teachings, this is especially vivid in John's writings although not so in our Western minds. We wrongly think we can love God with our head and not our heart, so we start asking if maybe God loves me but doesn't actually like me. We compartmentalize, but we do not learn this from Scripture. Rather we see in the Gospel of John that there is no abiding in truth apart from love, and no abiding in love apart from truth. We are not called to, or able to, abide in one and not the other.

Truth

The Hebrew concept of truth includes reliability and covenant faithfulness. The Greek is not so different. It embodies more than merely a statement that proves true rather than false. It is concerned with the truth Jesus shared verbally and showed, and all that the Spirit of truth would lead the disciples to remember and record. Truth involves doctrine, a word that simply means 'teaching.' Eternal truth is unchanging. To believe the truth means more than intellectual assent. In true belief our heart, mind, soul and body would embrace and embody truth.

The Gospel of John tells us that grace and truth come through Jesus (John 1:17), Jesus tells the truth (John 8:45), He bears witness to the truth (John 18:37), and is embodied truth revealing the Father (John 14:6). So in teaching us to abide in His words, Jesus was not encouraging us to look for new words, brand new just for me. He wants us to be saturated with that which He revealed, living in it, resting in it. God had been revealing truth in many ways. Through prophets but in these last days through his Son (Heb. 1:1-4). All that He revealed and has been recorded and which God has in His sovereignty protected through the centuries, we are to abide in. Abide, dwell, rest. Sit in it, bask in it, live in it.

As we abide in truth, truth abides in us, as a reading of John 14–15 will show. We first learn His words and embrace them with our whole being. Then we keep learning and never cease from learning. We do not reach a point at which a passage becomes stale, old, useless. We accept it over and over as lifegiving. We abide in His words that are powerful, that implant in our hearts, and that the Spirit will use to grow us, transform us, build us up, and increase our faith.

Abiding is the only way to be so saturated in the Word (in His truth, goodness and righteousness) that it shapes your reactions in this dark world. Self-effort cannot bring righteous knee-jerk reactions. Spirit led self-control comes from the Spirit, and abiding is how He calls us to it. Come unto Him and drink from the wellspring of life! And His life will flow into and out through you, all unto His glory.

Yet, how easy it is in the flesh to be led away from the simplicity and purity of abiding in Christ. Paul implores the Ephesians 'Let no one deceive you with empty words...' (Eph. 5:6). Empty words, vain words, worthless words, words that assure you that this covetousness is not so bad, words that convince you that God used to hate immorality, but now He understands that you did it in 'love' so it is okay. Words that justify your sin, your lust, your laziness. Words that allow you to believe you only need to hear a sermon and you will be full for the week. Words contrary to Scripture, which are the revealed words of God. We live in an age that is full of empty words. God's words are ' ... spirit and are life' (John 6:63). His words create, heal, redeem, refresh, renew, and are dripping with grace, mercy, peace, joy, and love.

Ephesians 5 continues by showing the distinct contrast between light and darkness. Verse 8 makes plain that apart from Christ we were darkness (also compare to Romans 6). Compare this to the opening prayer in Colossians that celebrates Christ rescuing us from the domain of darkness. Darkness in these passages signifies an inability to see or know God, in heart or mind or soul. Light is true knowledge. Intimate, intellectual, logical, pure knowledge. As part of the effects of sin, our hearts and minds cannot know God, or have a true knowledge of ultimate reality without the working of His Spirit in us. Light signifies this knowledge, and now describes us as light in the Lord. To be true to who God has created us to be we must walk in this light.

The fruit of the light in Ephesians 5:9 – goodness, righteousness, truth – is not the same as the Galatians list of fruits of the Spirit, but both are indeed works of the Holy Spirit. This is the fruit of knowing God, cultivated out of

God's truth abiding in us, and our abiding in His Word as His Spirit of truth leads and guides us. It is goodness. Deeds that are useful, helpful, generous and kind. It is righteousness, conforming to the character of God. It is truth, a life conforming to what is revealed and spoken in His Word, illumined to us by the eternal and unchanging Spirit. This fruit is produced in our lives not by law, nor self-effort, nor by the best study habits as we approach Scripture. It is not through trial and error or experimentation, seeing what works and what does not. It is the fruit of abiding, it is the fruit of gazing at the light of the world, who came to abide with us and in us. He abides in us, chasing the dark away. When we walk in the light, we expose the darkness for what it is rather than trying to approve it as light.

As you come to the Word, whether to read, study, meditate, or memorize, how do you come? Do you come trusting, seeking, desiring to know? Do you come in deed only, with your heart far off? Do you come as the Thessalonians did, expecting this to be not just empty words, but the power of God (see 1 Thess. 2:13)? God spoke in many ways, through many people, and in these last days through the Word incarnate (Heb. 1:1-4). These things were written for our instruction, perseverance and encouragement (See Rom. 15:4). As God's Word written, all of Scripture, and only Scripture, is God-breathed, and profitable for our entire life, not merely some compartment of our life (See 2 Tim. 3:16-17). And so, on these written words, whether read or heard as they are preached, we will feast and be constantly nourished, we will abide (See 1 Tim. 4:6-7). As Jesus spoke, people's hearts burned; His words were truly spirit and life (see John 5). We do not come as though to a magic book; we do not come as though to a book of formulas for life. We come knowing the Spirit will massage God's truth gently into our hearts, He will grant wisdom and knowledge, He will teach. What is written in Scripture cannot be used by us apart from the Spirit's work, as though we can send it forth on our own errands. We come to Him that we may have life. We continually come to Him for growth in understanding, for a flourishing, abundant life.

Love

The love which Christ shows us is another facet of what we are to abide in. We know what love is only if we look to the cross. 'We know love by this' says John, 'that [Jesus] lay down His life for us ...' (1 John 3:16). We do not know love primarily from any other source, it would be wrong to rewrite this verse inserting other sources of love. We do not know true love primarily from parents, spouses, friends as these relationships are imperfect and affected by sin. They ought to be saturated by love and when we are abiding in His love then the roles we play will display His love. But the love of the world is tainted by self and the deceitfulness of sin. Jesus, perfect sinless Jesus, has pure love for us. His love is not mingled with pride, selfishness, or lust. His love is everlasting. His love pursues without fail. His love endures, does not give up or pause or wait for us to be worthy.

The cross shows us that this love was given to us while undeserved. And His cross was not endured for the thanks we would render. We are frequently ungrateful, even on our best days. The cross shows us that love does not consider self but is concerned for the one loved. For God so loved the world. He loved, and acted, not for the sake of our loveliness, but out of His love. He does not tap into love, He is the source, the spring of love. The cross reminds us that God's love, which cannot be earned, is so rich that we cannot somehow overextend our need for it. Jesus' act on the cross was decisive and final. It is finished and we are secure.

We are sealed in His love, in His loving embrace. Nothing can separate us now. God does not change and His love does not change either.

In the Trinity, perfect love is enjoyed eternally. Looking through John 15:9 Jesus commands us to abide in His love, but just prior tells us that this love that He is calling us into is the same that the Father has for Him, the Son. The quality of that love is incomparable to human loves. Turning back to Isaiah 42:1 we are reminded that the Father says of the Son '... My chosen one *in whom* My soul delights.' His love is not stoic, it is a delighting love. He says 'My soul' to teach us that it is from all of His being. It is not separable from Him. Love Himself is the source of the love we abide in, and of the love that He pours into our hearts (see Rom. 5:1-5).

When Jesus was teaching His disciples how to love, He was clear that they were to love others in the very way that He had loved them. The Law had minimally taught them since Leviticus 19 to love others as themselves. Now in the Spirit they are led to love others more fully, loving them as Jesus loves. Jesus' love is richer and freer than any self-love. Disciples of Christ must not love as the world loves, not as people who scratch each other's backs love, not as fickle lovers. His love is different, fuller, deeper, selfless, and full of glory. His love is not borne of shared experiences, shared hobbies, shared opinions. He did not love you because you impressed Him or displayed loveliness. He is love, and in union with Him we are able to walk in God's supernatural (e.g. beyond mere nature), perfect love. We will stumble, we are not yet perfect, but we will not settle for the world's love. God delights in unchanging love. As we abide deeper in His love, we too will delight in unchanging love (see Micah 7:18).

Abide in His love, believing it, delighting in it, musing upon all He has revealed about His immense love that reaches to the heavens, and you will not be so easily swayed by lesser lovers. His love will fill you in such a way that it will saturate your whole being. Abiding in His love will lead to walking in love, speaking in love, and at the end of each day resting in His love. We will be content, knowing our perfect lover will never leave us, and that is enough.

His love is not merely fluffy feelings, but these are deep, true, feelings. The compassion of God is likened to that of a husband to his wife in Isaiah 54:4-10. If there is any doubt that husbands are meant to cherish their wives and express it fully, just spend some time in Song of Solomon. Let this then impact your reading of Hosea 11:8 (and indeed the whole of Hosea, as you see the Lord call to His bride). As you read of Jesus' emotional responses to life situations, think upon how His love abiding in you can impact your emotions. Emotions can be good servants as we experience life, but do not set them on the throne of your heart. Your heart's throne is a seat reserved for Jesus. Our love, our emotions, and our responses will be reshaped as we abide in God's love. Love sourced in ourselves will expect a return, will hold grudges, will expect forgiveness to be earned, will treat others the way they have treated us, will do no further kindness without being thanked. In Christ, in His love, we leave behind the world's love, and can finally love expecting nothing in return, we can forgive as Christ forgave us (forgiving before you or I even said sorry). We can heed His Word to love others as He has loved us.

When we abide in His love we do not look for people to fill us up. Rather we share His love, and we love expecting nothing in return. When we pursue sharing this life with other believers, the joy we can feel at being loved by them with this quality of love is incomparable. And sadly rare. Yet we abide in His love knowing we and our brethren cannot perfectly love. We do not give up on people who, like us, cannot perfectly love. We do not change our definition of love, or of fellowship, to suit this shortcoming. We forgive and seek Christ all the more.

To examine yourself, to see whether you are abiding in Christ's love, we do not merely look to actions. For even:

> If I speak with the tongues of men and of angels, but do not have love, I have become a noisy gong ... If I ... know all mysteries and all knowledge; and if I have all faith, so as to remove mountains, but do not have love, I am nothing. And if I give all my possessions to feed the poor, and if I surrender my body to be burned, but do not have love ... (1 Cor. 13:1-3).

It is quite possible to do loving actions, to be ever seeking ways to serve God and others, to make sacrifices for family and friends, but to have something other than God's love as your motivation. Such actions are worthless. They prove nothing, benefit no one, and do not glorify God. Apart from abiding in Jesus, in His Word and His love, we can do nothing of eternal value. Striving never produces spiritual fruit (see John 15:5-7).

Your First Love

We cannot do anything in order to find our way into God's love. He loved us first, drew us to Himself, and we felt drawn to seek Him. Yet the New Testament Epistles have many prayers for believers to be more loving, to be led further into His love, to walk in His love. His love will compel us, constrain us, and drive us toward loving actions. But imitating someone's actions or following a checklist of 'loving things to do' will not change your heart. His Spirit alone will pour out His love into our hearts (see Rom. 5:1-5) and out of that we live, and we act. The Ephesian church was once told that they had incorruptible love (see Eph. 6:24). Yet of the seven churches receiving letters via John in Revelation, we hear that the Ephesians have left their first love. When God calls them to repent, it is not merely a call to do more, it is a call primarily to abide once more in God's love, and then to let their actions be borne of love. Simply trying to play the part would not spark love in them. They are called to return. As we preach the gospel to our own souls, we quite often need to preach this word: return to Him, to your first love, to the one who loves you so perfectly and stands waiting to pour out His compassions on you.

'In Truth and Love'

John wrote to a particular church, as recorded in 2 John, saying they are those ' … whom I love in the truth …' and 'for the sake of the truth which abides in us …' (see 2 John 1–2). Have you had this attitude in you, toward the particular church God has placed you in? These people you worship with, fellowship with, share life with. Can you say that you love them in truth? According to God's truth, revealed in His Word? And for the sake of the truth? This harkens back to Jesus' prayer the night He was betrayed, that the love of the disciples for one another would give others confidence to trust the message they share (see John 17:20-23). In this letter John was not patronizing the church, this is God's love, shared amongst God's family. We cannot personally, or corporately abide in only truth, or only love. We abide in Christ. Chapter thirteen will focus on abiding together, so more on this will follow.

John continues his letter (2 John 7-11) by instructing the church to accept into their fellowship only those who abide in this teaching of Christ. To abide in this teaching will ultimately be to live in, to live from, to draw our strength and wisdom and knowledge from what Christ reveals. We share the gospel freely with the world, but those who deny it cannot become our teachers in life or godliness. We will not pick and choose which teachings we think are relevant but seek after all that God reveals in His Word and trust all that He said as good. Anyone who denies Christ's coming or His teachings shall not influence our worship, our conscience, our way of living. In another letter, John had written that anyone who knows God listens to the apostles' teaching, as they are the ones commissioned by Christ to bear witness to all they saw and heard while with Him (1 John 4:6). And so it is, when we immerse ourselves in Scripture, we are instructed to do all that we do in love, to walk in the truth, grow in knowledge, to be devoted to prayer, to extend love to one another in a myriad of ways and in these ways we walk in the light, manifesting the glory of God.

Practices

While Paul was discipling Timothy, he gave Timothy some beautiful instructions concerning Scripture in 1 Timothy 4. Sadly, many Christians dismiss this as 'friendly advice meant only for pastors,' when really it is also advice meant for a younger believer in the faith. We all ought to be teachers by now, teaching and encouraging and admonishing one another. So spend a few weeks in this Epistle. Re-read, journal, meditate on portions. Commit your heart to being '*constantly* nourished on the words of faith' (1 Tim. 4:6) rather than on snippets, or sound bites.

Journal through 1 Timothy 6:3. Meditate on what it means to know and desire this type of doctrine. Is this the desire of your heart?

Muse upon the themes of light and darkness from passages already mentioned and 2 Corinthians 3:15–4:6 and

Malachi 4:2. Journal through these Scriptures, use them to pray for yourself and your church, neighbors and family.

Slowly read through John chapters 6, 13–17. Write down the verses teaching about abiding and about what Jesus longs to give us, do for us, call us into. Read these chapters daily for a season and think upon them throughout your day. Soak them in, be nourished, let them marinate in your soul. Pray that God's desires would become your own as you put off lesser loves and non-truths.

To abide in love, we must make sure our definition of love is God's, and not the world's. Some of our biggest pains come from demanding or expecting 'love' that is not truly love. Some of our other pains come from those who do not have Christ's love dwelling in them, yet we expect them to love us well. Spend some time in prayer asking the Lord to help you learn to find all the love you need from Him, to forgive those who have hurt you, and show you ways to live in and from His love.

11

Abiding Deeper

The Spirit's work in us never ends, He will ever be drawing us deeper into the realities revealed by Christ, who is the Word made flesh. He will ever be enlarging our hearts and minds to know and enjoy Him more fully. The Word will never grow stale to those in union with Christ. We may have seasons of dark days, times when our souls feel disoriented. Our affections and thoughts are too scattered. We approach Scripture and stare, finding it difficult to read. Yet we hope in God, who will send out His light and His truth, (pause here to read Psalm 43).

> And now I commend you to God and to the word of His grace, which is able to build *you* up and to give *you* the inheritance among all those who are sanctified (Acts 20:32).

After one short visit, and another extended visit, Paul spoke these words while parting from the Ephesians. Did you notice all that Paul said the Word would do for these Christians? This Word of grace is working now, building up continuously. Working for our future, focusing our hearts on our secured inheritance. Building us up in strength, in fortitude, in steadfastness, in wisdom. Building up is common imagery in the New Testament:

> Therefore as you have received Christ Jesus the Lord, *so* walk in Him, having been firmly rooted *and now* being built up in Him and established in your faith, just as you were instructed, and overflowing with gratitude (Col. 2:6-7).

Being built implies that this work is ongoing, and passive. We are being built. We look to Him, gaze upon Him, delight in Him, listen to and believe Him. And look back to find ourselves further along in the faith.

The Glories of Christ

Ephesus was the capital of proconsular Asia when Paul taught in and wrote to the Ephesian church. It was the metropolis of a large region. A thoroughfare from East to West, a port city. Wealth and luxury were known within. Ephesus was home to the marble Temple of Artemis, one of the seven wonders of the ancient world. This city also had the largest of all Hellenic open-air theatres, which held a stadium used for races and wild-beast fights.

Ephesus was home to much idolatry, worshiping the goddess of propagation with orgies, practicing magic and sorcery, and famous for (and profiting from) its glitzy temple. In contrast to the wordly glory and false teachings of this city, Paul taught about the glory of God and the power of God's Word. He emphasized Jesus' love for His bride and the true mystery that is revealed, the knowledge and wisdom available to us in Christ.

Paul spent more time focusing on the glories of Christ. His goodness, His love, His beauty, His majesty and power, rather than detailing all that was wrong with magic, sorcery, temple prostitutes, idolatry, and the profit arising from these immoral acts. This is not because these things were not horribly wrong. They were, and the Ephesian Christians burned up a great amount of sorcery books in response. The Spirit was at work mightily. They did not keep their magic for entertainment, or to let loose after a hard day's work. After focusing on God's glory, they burned the very things they now recognized to be opposed to God's glory. In a culture that took a siesta in the middle of a hot day, they instead spent those hours learning from Paul. We, on the other hand, take a siesta and read books or watch movies very opposed to the glory of God, mock those who don't join in, and then wonder why our hearts stray so often. Some wonder if being steadfast in faith is real, if God's Word really does work mightily. But reading of Ephesus gives an example of God's Word at work, and of hearts becoming steadfast.

Through many thousands of years, many generations, and many false attempts at discovery, God's mystery was revealed! In Jesus, God has made known that which all the prophets desired to know, what all humanity longs for. His deeds and His words revealed that He was the true prophet, priest and king that we need and were created for. He showed the glory of His meekness as a suffering servant.

We are all searching, attempting to make meaning of our situations, of the world at large. In Christ we have the answers our souls long for and as we abide, this mystery becomes more clear. As we abide in His Word, He opens us up to know Him more, to grow in our knowledge of the world He created, and His plan to redeem His people, with plans to take us home to the new heavens and new earth. Read Colossians 1:25-28, and Romans 16:25-27. Paul was not speaking of a Gnostic mystery (some private knowledge), or cultic mystery that is only known by the initiated. Rather, this mystery is God's plan that was not yet revealed and now has been. His glorious purpose of redemption that was hidden until Christ made it known. Hence in Christ we are renewed to a true knowledge (Col. 3:10) but never apart from Christ.

Lifted

Every human attempt to discover God proves futile. His invitation is open, come to Him and find what you are looking for, find rest and wisdom and truth and every good thing. Even if one should come to His Word without coming to Him for understanding, that one will meet with disappointment. The hearts and minds of all are hardened towards Him since the fall. We have knowledge of good and evil and think it is sufficient. Unless Christ lifts the veil that separates us from God, unless He breathes life into our dead bones and change out our stony hearts, we will not know Him, or the reality of this world's situation. In Christ that veil is lifted, we see, and as we gaze upon Him beholding His glory, we become more human, more fully ourselves (read 2 Cor. 3:7-18). He spoke the world into existence, He speaks and all creation obeys. He has promised to send forth His Word to refresh, to fill us with joy and peace, to cause our flourishing (see Isa. 55 and John 14–16). He will speak to us in Christ, as we abide in His Word and keep His Word and cling to Him. He will cause the flourishing of our souls more deeply, more abundantly. Our inner man will flourish and rejoice, eagerly awaiting the glorious freedom we will more fully experience in heaven.

'… With perseverance we wait eagerly for it' (Rom. 8:25)! How often are believers said to be 'eager' in the Epistles? What are we to be eager for? Does your heart readily cry 'Come Lord Jesus' (Rev. 22:20)? The deeper your love and knowledge of Him grows, the more your faith will both feel and appear full of vigor. You will look to Him and be radiant, as Jesus Christ Himself is the radiance of God's glory. When we are weak, when we are in need of rest, we partake of the perseverance we find in Him, and our waiting is transformed by His peace and joy.

In the letter to the Colossians, Paul rejoiced to '... see your good discipline and the stability of your faith in Christ' (Col. 2:5). Discipline and stability appear to go hand in hand. This stability, or steadfastness, is the fruit of abiding not a spontaneous thing that pops up in our life. It is something we ought to pray for often, that '... the Lord direct [our] hearts into the love of God and into the steadfastness of Christ' (2 Thess. 3:5). This is not impossible for the Lord to work in our hearts, we ought to seek it eagerly. We ought to yearn for more, expectantly. Oh that we would have the discipline to seek Him, to know Him, to prayerfully listen to His Word, and to put off all that is contrary to this new man He is making us to be. When we are weak, He is our strength. When we are fickle, the God with whom there are no shifting shadows can make us steadfast. Lean upon Him, learn from Him, grow deeper with Him. The endurance, the fortitude, the depth of wisdom and knowledge, and the steadfast faith that He can work in us are real. And they are for every one of us, beloved.

Genuine, Steadfast, Fervent

This generation more than any other values transparency, vulnerability. But with this comes the possibility that we overtly focus on our sin and brokenness, which some pridefully sit in. 'I'm not okay, and I am okay with that' becomes the motto. This turns into 'I'll never be okay, leave me alone' and other variations on a theme that do not stem from the good news of Christ at work in us. Our motto ought to be 'what is impossible for me to accomplish is not impossible for God!' His Spirit ever flows, renewing and refreshing, making us more like Christ. He does not leave us as we came, though He does not work as instantaneously as our push-button culture demands. He knows our frame, and our situation. Therefore, at times He will speak to us as to Elijah, depressed in the cave and fleeing from enemies. At other times we will find God to be the gentle breeze that will calm and console and encourage. At times God will be our battle cry and the trainer of our hands for fighting for our faith. Other times, God's chastening will seem too severe, though afterwards we realize He was only cutting away idols and falsehood and rusty temporal trinkets. He is working to make us zealous for good works, more fervent in our love for His church, fervent in prayer, and steadfast in faith. And all to the praise of His glory, not ours. He heals. He teaches. He redeems. He is making all things new. He is bringing to completion the work He began. He is refining our faith (being both author and perfecter, see Heb. 12:2).

We ought to be more transparent about our need for God, our need for His church, our desire for His glory, and about the work He is doing in us when we sense it. We ought to be more vulnerable sharing burdens, sharing truth, and being faithful stewards of His gifts. We ought to be transparent about living out Romans 7, needing help from our source, and needing His truth to answer our doubts and fears. In this way we will experience true fellowship with one another, pointing each other to the reality of Christ's work and His being for us. When we seek validation for our situations from one another, we find a dead-end reward. We receive that validation, that glory from one another and we miss the grace God so desires to lavish upon us. In our desire to be transparent, let us seek Christ together, where and how He has taught us to. Let us point one another toward His Word and His love, and the confidence and boldness we have in Him. We ought to struggle against this world, rather than approving darkness, rather than merely validating others' opinion that life is hard and you should feel awful.

This deep abiding, clinging to the true vine for life, for fruitfulness, for the sap of joy and peace, this is not only for 'seasoned' believers, or those who seem naturally more meditative. This is for all people in union with Christ, His entire bride. We all ought to press on, that we may know Him, that we may grow in grace and knowledge, that we may find ourselves in Him (see Phil. 3). He has promised that ' ... the one who abides in love abides in God, and God abides in Him' (1 John 4:16) thus answering our fears of loneliness and purposelessness. He has also commanded:

> ... Let that abide in you which you have heard from the beginning. If what you heard from the beginning abides in you, you also will abide in the Son and in the Father. This is His commandment, that we believe in the name of His Son Jesus Christ, and love one another, just as He commanded us. The one who keeps His commandments abides in Him, and He in him ... (1 John 2:24; 3:23-24)

Twice on the night of Jesus' last meal with His disciples, Jesus said, 'do not let your heart be troubled,' (John 14:1,27) and He speaks this Word to us today. In the midst of whatever situation we are in, would He ever dismiss you to go off and be filled with despair, throw a tantrum and admit that you of all people have a right to be filled with angst, without hope? No. Do not let your heart pine away, but in your trouble, pray. He is with us, knowing our hearts are languishing and troubled. And He speaks hope, He gives peace, He promises a joy deeper than our circumstances. After a fuller explanation of the abiding Jesus is calling the disciples to, and giving commands to let His 'words abide in you' and to 'abide in [His] love' Jesus finishes with, 'These things I have spoken to you so that My joy may be in you, and *that* your joy may be made full' (John 15:11). As we cling (in heart, and mind), as we stay connected to our vine, we receive a foretaste of the heavenly joy He promised. We want that joy apart from tribulation. The disciples still faced Roman law, Pharisaical heresies, false gods of all the neighboring communities, fear of physical punishment and death, and utter loneliness should families disown them. Could they relate to your situation? Can Jesus? Yes, beloved, you are not alone or unique in your struggles and Jesus' joy can be made full in you because His joy is not mere emotion. His joy is not linked to circumstances. It is not pretending we live in heaven now. It is not a striving after our best life now. We have a better, eternal, ultimate inheritance awaiting us; therefore we need not struggle for temporal dreams and ideologies to make us happy. It is abiding in His words and His love, knowing He abides in you and fills you, even now, that will cause this joy to shine forth in your heart.

The simplicity of devotion to Christ will greatly impact your experience of His joy. It is quite commonly a 'multiplicity' of heart devotions that cause our true love, our hope, and our joy to wane. In simplicity, or singlemindedness we admit we cannot have it all, do it all, or play all the roles. We walk away from the idea that jobs or resumes or trophies or hobbies or possessions define us and make us who we are. One by one, in His mercy, He will show you that which distracts your heart from simplicity. There is a vast difference between owning and enjoying His good gifts and being owned by them. In simplicity, we enjoy everything as a gift, we enjoy our role as stewards basking in God's glory (not our own).

In Christ, we have freedom to walk in His joy, which implies letting go of distractions. Those distractions cause little sparks in our brains, fooling us into letting them take hold of us. Then begins addiction. We think we are using things only to discover that we are being controlled. Let go of filling too many roles, owning too many possessions, or signing up for too many activities that demand your devotion. Sometimes the seeds of distraction we planted have taken deep root in our hearts and letting go requires help, pastoral counseling, a spiritual mentor, a therapist or licensed professional counselor. Brothers and sisters in Christ ought to help one another in this – praying, admonishing, encouraging, using our gifts as we can. Maturing in our spirituality means we will seek the help we need from those who will point us ultimately to the help we have in Christ alone.

Brethren, cling to Him alone, make your boast in Him alone. We let go too often of the simple quiet life He calls us to because we long for earthly satisfaction, earthly fame, earthly titles. We do not want to depend on others as a body is created to do. We want all the spiritual gifts so we do not have to live in harmony with the community. Preach to your soul rather to long for that which really satisfies, and to seek after the simplicity and purity of devotion to Christ alone.

Wisdom for the Mature

While Scripture tells us that not many who are wise in worldly wisdom come to know the Lord, Scripture also demands that those who do know Him will not stay simpletons in heavenly wisdom. The Word of the cross appears foolish to those steeped in secular wisdom, but to us who are Christians that very Word is the power of God, both to redeem and to renew (see 1 Cor. 1:18-25). His power that accompanies the Word of the cross is not stagnant, allowing us to remain as is.

The wisdom He gives freely grows us. There will always be more to learn and delight in, to rest in, to savor and ponder, more to aspire to and seek out. We ought to desire God's wisdom, and delight to be among the mature. He satisfies us in the depths of our hearts, and as He does He awakens deeper desires within us that lead us to enjoy all that we can while sojourning here. We ought to come back for long steady draughts of the rivers of living water as we await the pleasures that are at His right hand forevermore!

1 Corinthians 2 teaches about this special working of the Spirit, which flourishes in those who are spiritually minded. Our faith finds its true seat in the power of God, when our faith is fed by hearing the Word. No other source will do (see 1 Cor. 2:4-5). If He abides in you, the Spirit will be teaching you from the 'depths of God' (1 Cor. 2:10). Abiding in Him will make available to you true spiritual thoughts. These thoughts do not come through your own efforts in philosophizing, or pondering nature, or reading great books (though these are wonderful vocations). These thoughts are from the depths of God's wisdom and knowledge and are given by and through the Spirit alone.

Romans 8 also teaches us about the wisdom for the mature as Paul reminds us of our role in obedience. We set our minds upon the Spirit, rather than the flesh. As the flesh competes for our affections this will be difficult, but not impossible. We are yielding to God's working in us, we are not alone. We are not earning anything through obedience, we are rather participating. As we participate we enjoy the blessings of that obedience. We set our minds on the Spirit and then enjoy His peace. But we do not dare set our minds upon the Spirit without listening to Him. The Spirit takes all that God has spoken and gives it to us, granting understanding. To set the mind on the Spirit is to prayerfully, humbly, abide in the

Word. The Spirit wields His sword which is the Word of God (see Eph. 6:17). As we abide we can heed the call also to be wise in what is good. We can agree with God in what He calls good, we can delight in His pleasures that cause flourishing in our souls. We can respond to temporal situations by acting in faith, that our obedience would be known to all, the obedience of faith (see Rom. 1:5-6; 16:19, 25-27).

Practices

Read a book on biblical theology. J.I. Packer wrote a beautiful essay as an introduction to John Owen's, *Death of Death in the Death of Christ,* which I believe would encourage all believers. It is a good read as you begin or refresh your study of biblical theology.

A few other suggested readings:

Clowney, Edmund, *Mystery Revealed.*
Ferguson, Sinclair, *The Christian Life.*
Voss, Geerhardus, *Biblical Theology.*

Commit John 17:3 to memory and come back to it often and prayerfully. Read the whole of Jesus' last teachings in John 13–17 during times of rest (perhaps a perfect Sabbath day reading). Each time find new promises to pray through, and verses to cling to. Consider Jesus' own attitude toward the Old Testament, study it, and seek to grow in the same appreciation for all that God reveals therein.

Find all the New Testament passages detailing what we ought to be devoted to (use a concordance). Journal through these with ideas and prayers for seeking God's help in being devoted, and in having your desires aligned with His. Pray through 2 Timothy 1:6-7, 13-14 for yourself as you work through this.

Philippians 4:4-9 directs us to 'dwell' on certain things. This text deserves to be studied. Set aside time to pay attention slowly to each verse, each verb, each promise or command. Study closely and linger as you do. Journal a list of possible 'whatevers' from verse 8. Journal a list of the things mentioned in verse 9. Commit to returning to this passage weekly and meditating on these things. In moments of despair, angst, anxiety, or stress, because you have spent the time dwelling, you will be able to set your mind on these things when you desperately need peace and renewal. Obeying in the easy times, the times you choose to set aside, will create a path in your mind easier to travel down in the chaotic times. Stress and anxiety creep in, but the honorable, the true, the lovely, the pure, the good, the thoughts truly worthy of your time and attention that you have been abiding in will help you fight, help you endure and exult. And if you are mindful, you'll notice that the God of peace abides with you through the storms of life.

Meditate on Psalm 36:5-11. Ponder each image presented. Write out a prayer in your journal based on these promises and beautiful declarations.

12

Nothing Apart from Abiding

Apart from abiding in Christ, we can do nothing. Nothing. Not one thing of eternal value. Yes, we can set routines, set goals, make five-year plans, buy and sell and earn, make a name for ourselves, eat drink and be merry. But, apart from abiding in Christ we cannot cause flourishing in our lives or the lives of others. We cannot strive to make or do anything of real value. We end up causing only shadows, molding only mud puddles. And sometimes, the world, our flesh and the devil put up such a good fight, that on our own we cannot even strive after 'goals, routines, plans,' or even get out of bed. Our flesh will fail us, our strength will run dry.

While embracing the truth of our humanity, we will admit we are weak and that we have limited time here on earth. Our life here on earth is but a vapor, a mist, a fog quickly evaporating. Facing that fact, knowing that, we ought to take seriously the call to abide and not save it for another day. While it is still called today let us succumb to His drawing us closer, let us enjoy His promise to be our lifegiving vine. Daily we need to remind ourselves of the beauty of this relationship, and we need to rest in it.

In John 15:1, 3-5 we read the call and promise:

> I am the true vine, and My Father is the vinedresser. You are
> already clean because of the word which I have spoken to you.
> Abide in Me and I in you. As the branch cannot bear fruit of
> itself unless it abides in the vine, so neither *can* you unless
> you abide in Me. I am the vine, you are the branches; he who
> abides in Me and I in him, he bears much fruit, for apart from
> Me you can do nothing.

Our fruit are not mere accomplishments or checklists. Our fruit will primarily be soul virtues, the reality of becoming like Christ, and in so doing acting like Him toward others. Loving others as He loved us. His love constrains believers.

His love re-orients our affections, our reason, our will. As we abide, we will imitate Him in word and deed (Eph. 5:1-2; Col. 3:17; 1 John 3:18). To be drawn into the steadfast, unchanging love of Christ and to abide in it implies musing upon it, thinking, imagining, singing of it, believing it is deeper and wider than any ocean I see (Eph. 3:18-19), and believing He longs to fill my heart with more love than I can comprehend. We must take the time to ponder this regularly, it is how we let '… Christ dwell in our hearts through faith, … being rooted and grounded in love' (Eph. 3:17).

Believing I can do nothing apart from Him will not cause despair. It is a glorious freedom He has called us into. Freedom from condemnation, from despair, from the world's labels, from my own limited abilities. I am free to thrive and flourish as a fruitful branch, having the all-satisfying eternal life flowing from the vine into me. Free to thrive, though still living in a world tainted by the fall, full of tribulation and sadness and death. I thrive when I remember that this world is not my home, I am but a sojourner here.

In Him We Are Clean

The promise in Jeremiah 33:8 is fulfilled in Christ, He has cleansed us from all that defiles and makes us impure. We are clean because of the Word He has spoken. Just as powerfully as Jesus saying 'hush, be still' to a storm, by the Word of His power He has cleansed us from our sin. Jeremiah's promise includes our cleansing, and God's intent to ever be revealing His peace and truth, and oh how beautifully they fit together!

Christ willingly became flesh, and became our sin, He took our filthy rags. He bore our reproach on the cross. And it is finished. We bear no more shame, no more guilt, no more condemnation. We are no longer under the jurisdiction of the law but are justified by grace. We walk now as new creatures, and being His new creation is all that matters (see Gal. 6:15). We take hold of the eternal life to which we were called and we now walk in the Spirit's leading. We await with eager anticipation the white robe that will be ours in heaven.

As we abide and so crucify the flesh or put to death the deeds of the flesh, we look to the Word of the cross. We look to all that Jesus' death and resurrection accomplished on our behalf. Though He has cleansed our conscience and made us new we still war with our old man, the flesh, and the world. We oppose everything that is in opposition to God's glory. Romans 4 reminds us that He died for our justification and was raised for our sanctification. So to be fruitful, to abide in the cleansing and sanctifying work He is doing we ponder the cross and the resurrection. We meditate on the Gospels, Acts, and other key Scriptures such as 1 Corinthians 15. As we immerse ourselves in these particular truths, our minds will grow in grasping the power and sovereignty that is His alone. And the world's words that seek to destroy us will lose their power. We are cleansed from the defiled flesh that was ours and understand what it means to be made new. The lusts and over-powering desires that were once ours, that once reigned over us and that are opposed to God's glory, can no longer control us. They do not define us; we are cleansed from their power over our thoughts, affections, and actions.

When we ponder 'For you have died and your life is hidden with Christ in God' (Col. 3:3) we begin to further understand that we did not know ourselves rightly apart from knowing Him. Our creator and sustainer can reveal who we are. While we can try to make something of ourselves, we will not do so very successfully. He created us for a purpose, He created us with 'good works' in mind. Unique in that way, we cannot look around at our friends as the pattern for living. We end up in envy, competing with one another, and frustrated that His gifts to us are not the same as what others have received.

We gaze at Christ, find our life hidden in Him, and listen to Him and follow Him as only His sheep can (John 10:27). We cease striving to make the world love us, or to be our own separate plant. We delight more and more to abide as a branch in the true vine. We are cleansed and we are continually abiding. Then comes obedience, faith working through love, and the joy and peace that only accompanies believing(Rom. 15:13).

In Him We Are Enriched

In Christ we have everything! We are told to 'consider our calling' remembering that though we were foolish and weak, He has become to us wisdom, righteousness and sanctification (1 Cor. 1:26-31). 'Sanctification' implies of course that we are in process, always becoming more like Christ, always becoming more of who He created us to be, becoming more real. In 1 Corinthians 3:18-23 we also hear of our being foolish and weak apart from Him. Taking the time to consider all of this will be both enriching and renewing to our souls. Enriched in all things, ready to walk in His purposes and callings. Enriched to build upon the foundation with gold, silver and precious jewels rather than wood and hay that would burn up easily (1 Cor. 3:5-15). You will not know what the gold, silver, and truly valuable building supplies are on your own. He delights in our prayers, asking to have all our needs supplied; and He delights to enrich us for all the good works He calls us to.

We are mistaken if we believe this means we do not feel any need. Our needs should help us press deeper into fellowship with God and our work will be for God's glory and our good. We were created for this, called into this, and as abiding branches we are enriched for this. The more you abide in Him, and believe you have nothing apart from Him, the more you will understand true contentment. '... being content with what you have, for He Himself has said "I WILL NEVER DESERT YOU, NOR WILL I EVER FORSAKE YOU"' (Heb. 13:5). This verse doesn't mean much to a believer who finds worth in the material world alone, or who struggles to believe Jesus cares about us on all levels. We will have troubles; we will still face life every day in a fallen world. Yet, we live knowing we are never apart from God and He gives our life meaning and eternal value.

Abiding in Him, we will gladly acknowledge that everything we have and are comes from Him. From God, through God, and to God are all things (Rom. 11:36) whether the air in our lungs, the affections of our hearts, the ideas filling our minds, the physical provisions and daily bread for our bodies. In Him we find the wholeness that humanity lost in the garden. Apart from Him we are naked and longing to be clothed. He clothes us in His righteousness. Apart from Him we are ashamed, hiding, weary from effort, and disillusioned with earthly life. He finds us, takes away our shame, strengthens and enlivens us, and enlightens our understanding. The curse makes us look upon ourselves alone. He takes away our curse that we may lift our gaze to see Him, know Him, and enjoy the foretaste of what we've always been looking for.

In Jesus, who is the way, the truth and the life, full of wisdom and knowledge, we can 'do' and 'be' according to God's design. This abiding is constant, moment by moment, conscious and subconscious. He gives life to our whole being, enriching every aspect of heart, mind, soul, and strength. At first, as we are little children in the faith, it seems to take great effort to turn our attention toward Him, to be mindful of His constant presence and power in our lives. It takes effort to set our minds on the Spirit, on the Word, on Christ above. But as we grow in this and our minds are trained, our thoughts will easily be guided along these ancient paths with less effort. We need to constantly walk through the process of being renewed or taking off the old and putting on the new.

In Him We Are Fruitful

We are, and we will be fruitful. What is this fruit? Not the checklist you may think of, not a list of accomplishments or even tangible goods you can point to. Our fruit will not be something we boast of, 'look what I did!' Rather, we will boast only in the cross of Christ, and of His working in and through us. Our fruit will be primarily in our heart, in our inner man, spilling out to bless those we are in relationship with. Our fruitfulness will impact the community we are a part of, it will not be self-serving. Our fruitfulness begins as we trust that abiding in Him leads to discovery of our true self, hidden in Christ. We lean into Him for this knowledge. When we quit running to jobs or duties or possessions in order to feel good or whole or valuable and when we run to

Christ alone, then we will be fruitful. We will become more like Him and experience the purposes He has for our life. In Ephesians we hear that He has had good works set aside for us to walk in (Eph. 2:10). He creates us anew, and we are finally able to fulfill our true vocation, being fruitful in ways that are eternally good and useful. When you hear 'vocation' do not think 'way of earning money.' Life is so much more than money. Earning money in this world is only a fraction of the will of God for any person's life. Some of our most important fruit will stem from our free time activities.

These are the greater works Jesus spoke of while teaching His disciples about their future (See John 14:12). While calming their anxiety about His leaving them and reassuring them of the wonder of life in the Spirit, Jesus taught His disciples that by walking in the Spirit, having the Spirit as teacher and comforter and guide, they would be part of His kingdom work producing greater fruit. Apart from Him, we are impotent; but in Him the fruit is beyond our imagining greater than we could otherwise think of or do. Children of God will learn from Him, and imitate Him and are enabled to be truly, beautifully, fruitful.

Go back and read the covenant promises in Jeremiah 33. God says He will reveal to His children an abundance of peace and truth. This is the very same idea that Paul conveys to the Philippians, that God will guard our hearts and minds in His peace as we dwell on what is true. We will be fruitful in heart and mind, in word and deed, as our inner man is renewed. In Him, our fruits are greater than any temporal plans or dreams.

'Apart from Me you can do nothing' (John 15:5). Have you yet begun to believe that you need Him for everything? That in abiding in Him, you receive His promised Spirit? The Holy Spirit empowers us, fills us, leads us into truth, guides us, gives us understanding and wisdom. Once we walk in the Spirit we begin to wonder why we ever tried to do life apart from Him. And we become more thankful, knowing God has been ever so patient with us. How can we keep ourselves in this path, or as Jude says (see verse 21), to keep ourselves in the love of God? Paul says he dies daily, and having died with Christ, the life he leads is richer, fuller, full of His glory. Never will an earthly day go by that we do not need Him. We continue to be fruitful when we determine to press on in the same manner as Paul, abiding deeper.

One enemy to our fruitfulness that we will face daily is our own flesh. Galatians 5:17 reminds us that the desires of the Spirit and flesh are against one another. Indeed, it is our own surface level desires that keep us from doing the things that we deep down, in our heart that is new, want to do. Flesh and Spirit are opposed to one another and will never be in step. Thus, circumcision, or law keeping for sanctification sake, is not of the Spirit. To attempt orchestrating our own sanctification will keep you back from living the abundant life Christ has called you to. The abundant life is what you want deep down, though your flesh is too easily appeased by less (see 2 Cor. 3:18).

Though we are clean, enriched, and fruitful, yet (see John 16:33) we will have tribulation until He takes us home. We are called, according to Peter, to suffer with Jesus. We have walked away from sin and lusts and worldly ways seeking fulfillment, but we cannot separate ourselves from the troubles of this world. We enjoy this mutual abiding still, especially in our tribulations. We do not all face the same sufferings, but our needs in the midst of them are the same. We must cling to Jesus through our sufferings to experience His endurance. Let go of Him and troubles will consume us. We would falter and suffer shipwreck to our faith. We would walk away from the simplicity and purity of knowing Him, loving Him, and keeping in step with His Spirit.

Apart from Him we cannot even pray. John 15:7-8 tells us to abide in Him, and His words abide in us, and then we pray. Whether it be your first prayers in response to the gospel, 'help me Jesus!' or even the more seasoned prayers offered up in the midst of the mundane or in response to troubled times, we learn to pray as we abide. There is no abiding apart from prayer, even if we cannot find words to express the prayer. And let us not forget the promise that when we cannot find the words, the Spirit Himself groans from within us, praying a prayer too deep for words (Rom. 8:22-27). Remembering this promise has helped me through many a weary season. When we pray from a posture of abiding, the assurance dawns upon our hearts that we are in tune with Him. The Spirit helps us pray in those times when it seems too hard to pray. As you read and internalize His words, let that reading fuel your prayers. In this way, our hearts are strengthened by His grace, and not by uttering a wish list of fleshly temporal desires to our cosmic Santa. Jesus taught His disciples how to pray, we heed those same words. To pray as He taught His disciples, we too pray with His words abiding in us, this is how we pray in the Spirit (see Jude 19-20 and Eph. 6:17-18). True prayer is not merely giving vent to your feelings. We pour out our hearts before Him most honestly when we pray in harmony with the Word. Cling to the Word of life and let that direct your prayers. Let His words distill your heart, inform your mind, inflame your affections, and let His words linger in your heart as you pray. Trust not in your own understanding (Prov. 3:1-8) as you pray. Acknowledge Him, your need for Him, your desire for His glory and power and goodness. He delights in those who abide in Him, think upon that as you set your heart to pray.

In Him We Are Full

We need not strive to fill in any gaps, His work is sufficient. In this life of mutual abiding, He will fill us, provide for every good work He calls us to, and complete His own work in us. We walk with Him as He works. We obey and follow as He teaches us to. But it is He who teaches, and we must heed His call to listen. Apart from Him we are nothing, but as His vessels who are used for His glory, He will fill us.

> For it was the *Father's* good pleasure for all the fullness to dwell in Him, and through Him to reconcile all things to Himself, having made peace through the blood of His cross; through Him, *I say*, whether things on earth or things in heaven.
>
> And although you were formerly alienated and hostile in mind, *engaged* in evil deeds, yet He has now reconciled you in His fleshly body through death, in order to present you before Him holy and blameless and beyond reproach–if indeed you continue in the faith firmly established and steadfast, and not moved away from the hope of the gospel that you have heard, which was proclaimed in all creation under heaven, and of which I , Paul, was made a minister. (Col. 1:19-23).

Some will read this passage and focus solely on the 'if.' This passage is misused by some with a faulty emphasis on our need to be steadfast, holy, blameless, beyond reproach. But it is Christ's work to reconcile us, as well as to make us holy, to take our blame, and make us beyond reproach. As we look to Christ, abiding in Him, we have glimpses of how He is doing this but it is Christ working in us, for us, on our behalf. We remain steadfast in the same manner that we abide in Him. It is not a complicated work; it is the simplicity of faith. It is believing His work, it is believing His words, and trusting that He will complete the work begun in us. This passage should not knock us down with the weight of impossible work. It should draw us to keep our eyes on Christ our

King. It should spur us on to desire His kingdom, to humbly submit to His reign in our hearts, and to long for our life that is hidden in Him. As we do, there will be an ever-increasing delight in His words that call us to obedience. And we will obey, though not yet perfectly, as we are motivated by His love, out of the fullness that He has poured into our hearts.

Outside of abiding, all our efforts, our love, our plans, our every intention will be tainted by flesh. Apart from abiding, even our prayers will just be our flesh crying out, and not the 'praying in the Spirit' that we learn about in Scripture (remember, Eph. 6 and Jude). Know God's Word, and you can pray in tune with it; pray in the Spirit and it will be true prayer indeed. As you grow in this practice of praying in the Spirit, or praying from a posture of abiding, your experience of His joy and peace will increase.

Practices

Commit John 15:5 to memory.

Consider God's eternal desire to bring us into lives of flourishing. Read through Isaiah 30, Isaiah 48, and Ezekiel 16. He knows your heart and knows when you are languishing. He knows how to bring you out of languishing into flourishing.

Journal through Philippians 3:1-14, slowly. Take a few days to ponder each idea, asking the Holy Spirit to work in you this 'pressing on' mindset.

Consider Paul's instructions to Timothy in 1 Timothy 1:11-21 and 2 Timothy 1:13-14. What does Paul say will be helpful to Timothy for growth in the faith? Take note of the glory given to God, muse upon the doxology found here, and work it into your own prayer life. Note the emphasis upon the obedience we are called to being fulfilled 'through the Holy Spirit who dwells in us …' Read this in light of what

Jesus teaches in John 13-16 about abiding in Him, and His abiding in us.

Dedicate a season of life, perhaps a month in length, to practice incorporating Romans 6:19 into your prayer life. Imagine a scene in which you are presenting your heart, your mind, your will, your physical body. Lay a few things down at His cross as the Spirit brings them to mind (pride, envy, grumbling). Release the things He has freed you from (striving, worry, insecurity, doubt). After a season of intentionally practicing this, it will become an automatic part of your prayer life, opening your day.

> I am speaking in human terms because of the weakness of your flesh. For just as you presented your members as slaves to impurity and to lawlessness, resulting in *further* lawlessness, so now present your members as slaves to righteousness, resulting in sanctification (Rom. 6:19).

Pray as David did in Psalm 131, having composed and quieted your heart – by focusing on who God is, on His steadfast love, on the beauty of His holiness, and the perfection of His goodness and glory. Compose and quiet your soul by silencing the lies and doubts and worries that creep in. Hold them up to the word of His power and let them fade away. He will keep you in His peace and guard your heart and mind.

Journal through these verses: Jeremiah 33:6-9; John 14:27; John 15:11; John 16:33; John 17:13. Pray for God's promises and desires to become the overwhelming desires of your own heart.

13

Abiding Together

When God calls someone into union with Christ, it is as part of His body. His body has many members, you are but one of them. You are called into fellowship with God and with His family, His children. You were not called to be alone, you were set into a kingdom full of priests with whom there is to be mutual upbuilding. There is no distinction of value among persons in this body, we are called to enjoy fellowship with all believers, with all who call upon Him in truth.

Here and now we are called to enjoy this fellowship, already mentioned in 1 John. The unity Jesus desires for us currently He fervently prayed for in John 17. But as seen in all the directives given to early churches, this plays out in a particular church, where you live life amongst particular believers. Peter speaks to new believers in this way:

> Since you have in obedience to the truth purified your souls for a sincere love of the brethren, fervently love one another from the heart, for you have been born again not of seed which is perishable but imperishable, *that is*, through the living and enduring word of God. (1 Pet. 1:22-23).

Being born again included being born into this community of brethren. God spoke, and you were born again of His Word. He speaks life into us and into this community (also read Rom. 10:14-17). The great work that God has done is not merely to keep us from facing His wrath, but in reconciling us to Himself God creates peace among us. We find ourselves in His community of love. Therefore, we ought to fervently love one another from the heart. With all we have and all we are and all we can muster. This love is active, all encompassing, and full of passion. This love is not selective, or partial, or exercised in an attitude of favoritism. To act in favoritism is to '... blaspheme the fair name by which you have been called' (James 2:7).

Within our particular community we grow in our love for the Lord, and for His people. Many New Testament passages remind us that without loving the brethren, we cannot love the Lord. The most obvious teaching is found in 1 John: if you cannot love a person you see, then you cannot love God whom you do not see. Sometimes the problem with our love, is that once we catch a glimpse of the gospel light, we want to share that with those outside the community, and we do not partake in actual fellowship within the church. To this, Paul spoke directly:

> So then, while we have opportunity, let us do good to all people, and *especially* to those who are of the household of faith (Gal. 6:10).

> Now as to the love of the brethren, you have no need for *anyone* to write to you, for you yourselves are taught by God to love one another; for indeed you do practice it toward all the brethren who are in all Macedonia. But we urge you, brethren, to excel still more (1 Thess. 4:9-10).

140

Especially who? Is there really an especially? Yes there is, we are commanded to love the brethren especially. Sometimes we get tunnel vision and love only our family. Or only our close friends who have such similar likes and dislikes. Or we have no loving relationships and seek only to give time and energy to showing Christ's love to unbelievers. The Spirit directed the church to focus on loving the brethren, and this Word is for the church in all generations. It is then into this mutual love that we can invite unbelievers. How can we experience Christ's love apart from His means? He meant for us to enjoy fellowship with God and others. Those others are His hands and feet in our lives. He called us into a kingdom of love. When we abide in His love, it will bubble out into the community we are invested in. We will be stewards of His grace as we actively love, in word and deed, those in our particular church. We cannot grow in love while living in isolation from the brethren. We grow together.

> ... but speaking the truth in love, we are to grow up in all *aspects* into Him who is the head, even Christ, from whom the whole body, being fitted and held together by what every joint supplies, according to the proper working of each individual part, causes the growth of the body for the building up of itself in love (Eph. 4:15-16).

Every member of Christ's body adds to the growth of His body, and all members need the other members. I cannot grow in isolation, neither can you. We cannot abandon His body and imagine we are pleasing God. We cannot walk away from scriptural teaching on fellowship believing we've found a new or better way.

All Week Long

True fellowship cannot happen in a church where members come and go on Sundays but are never known by other members, never welcomed as important or where members never engage in spiritual conversations, serving, or getting to know others. Many people walk away from churches when all of this is not felt on a Sunday morning. But everything in its season, in its time, in its place. Sunday morning is rightly designed for worshiping God together. So the 'one another' ways in which we engage in loving and serving each other must happen the rest of the week. We cannot blame others for not loving us, if we are not intentionally, fervently, loving people in our particular local church. We cannot wait for the right moment when we feel needed, appreciated, or desired. For then we are not loving while 'expecting nothing in return' (Luke 6:27-36). We all ought to value God's glory above all else, but our hunger for earthly glory (thanks and recognition) controls us and diminishes our enjoyment of fellowship with others who are also created in His image. If we abide in His love, then we dare not demand to be loved in a certain way. We set our hearts and minds to accept one another just as we were accepted by God (while still sinners) and love one another as Christ did (not self-serving, giving without thinking of what I gain by it). A program will not make this happen, flesh and blood will not manufacture this. Fervent love such as is spoken of in the Gospels and Epistles cannot be programmed, but we do have a responsibility to walk in this love.

Growth, Together

So how do we do this, without a program? Begin by musing on the Scriptures, perhaps 1 Thessalonians 3:11-13. Though in our Western Christianity we think too individualistically, there is in actuality no holiness apart from fellowship! God's love is perfectly directed toward all His children, and into this love we are called. Can we share it? Can we abide together in it? We need to, and we ought not to take it for granted. '... Pursue righteousness, faith, love, *and* peace, with those who call on the Lord from a pure heart' (2 Tim. 2:22). Pursue these together, because we were not meant to go it alone. Creating an ethos where we feel free to ask for prayer, ask for help, share what we are learning, and speak truth into one another's lives will take time and intention. It will be intentional, organic ministry rather than merely a program.

Paul laments the times when he looked around to realize that many so-called Christians abandoned him and the work of the Church. Paul's pain was real and will be shared by many until Christ takes us home. This experience is part of the suffering we face here, as there are no perfect churches. There are no perfect Christians. The tares will not be removed from the wheat field until Christ brings in the harvest.

Though the pain of broken fellowship is acute, the joy and peace that stem from true fellowship is worth the risk. Does this make you want to look for people with similar hobbies and interests? Or will you look for friends who call upon the Lord from a pure heart? Do you stray from the simplicity and purity of devotion to Christ by seeking friends the world's way? Many believe we need fellowship with others who share the exact same situations. The result is a church fragmented into classes and groups. When your fellowship is fragmented you miss what God intended for His body. We need other generations alongside us. Are you the kind of person who could be sought out for this true fellowship? A pure heart, one that calls upon Christ alone, is that your heart's desire? The happiness offered in shallow, temporal friendship cannot compare to the joy of friendship with those who say, 'One thing I have asked ..., and that I will seek ...' (Psalm 27:4). The former will flit from season to season finding new associates, the latter will cling to Christ and so be committed to those in their local body. To abide in Him, in His words, in His love, also includes sharing His Word and His love with each other. We pursue these things together prayerfully, in light of all His Word teaches. The fellowship and friendship that follow are what Paul describes in Ephesians, that we are '... being fitted together, is growing into a holy temple in the Lord ... being built together into a dwelling of God ...' (Eph. 2:21-22).

Mutual Aid

God comforts in all our afflictions, and as the God of all comfort He alone gives true comfort (see 2 Cor. 1:1-11). Unless we are abiding in His words and love, we cannot know or share this deep comfort. But while abiding, we can and we must share; we are His hands and feet to one another. We weep together, we wipe tears, we encourage and strengthen, we hug and accept and help. And He has deemed that our endeavors would spread His comfort, the only true, deep, comfort. This comfort, this peace and wellbeing amidst a life of tribulation, is not the same as what the world offers – God's comfort is effective, lasting, beyond comprehension and yet grasped and known by His own. When we abide in His comfort having received it during any of our own afflictions, we are less inclined to speak words to one another out of fear or from the desire to apply quick fixes. We speak His grace, His balm, in season. We do not mix in judgment of why a situation occurred as we may never have the wisdom to know. We must not speak out of mere worldly experiences, or from the knowledge of good and evil, but rather out of knowing Him who is true, knowing His words of eternal life, and knowing Him who is making all things new. We forgive flippant words, knowing He has forgiven me of much more. Yet we must speak words of comfort in season. Some fear speaking because of the harsh attitude others have vented, some wrongly believe that to speak comfort we must have gone through all the same details of all the same situations. The prayers and words of comfort from our fellow brethren can point us to the God of all comfort; we are not alone. Pride and flesh will refuse comfort and separate us; His love will unite us.

Mutual aid will be shared as we walk in the Spirit. Paul outlines some of the pitfalls the Galatians experienced in chapter five of that Epistle. He also, by inspiration of the Spirit, shows the beauty of life lived in step with His Spirit. The flesh leads to ruin and destruction as we challenge one another, envy, or boast, and eventually devour one another. The life lived in the Spirit is filled with His fruit of love, kindness, and everything good that will cause flourishing in our fellowship. When we walk in the Spirit, then as the Colossians were instructed, we will speak and even sing of God's grace, and love, and glory. We will not keep silent, we will not leave one another to suffer alone. We will also not devour the hand that delivers the words of grace we so desperately need.

True Fellowship

If we gather but our thoughts are never turned towards Christ then we have not engaged in fellowship. We share something wonderful, yet because of the fragmented society we have grown up in, we fear sharing eternal things, soul things. It is completely unnatural and yet because it is so unnatural it will be all the more wonderful if you do engage. It will be of the Spirit. As we abide in His words, and pray in the Spirit, and continue in the Spirit, these words we abide in will be shared and delighted in.

Peter, who instructed the churches scattered in several cities, taught us to love one another fervently from the heart. He also detailed in that same letter a few points on how to carry this out.

> To sum up, all of you be harmonious, sympathetic, brotherly, kindhearted, and humble in spirit; not returning evil for evil or insult for insult, but giving a blessing instead; for you were called for the very purpose that you might inherit a blessing (1 Pet. 3:8-9).

Notice how selfless this sounds? The focus is never on what I will get from the persons I fellowship with, for my blessing is my inheritance, all of which is in heaven where nothing can touch it. Yet, if this logically plays out, then you rest from striving after selfish things because other members of the body care for you, whilst you care for them. Mutual upbuilding. He continues with his focus on fervency:

> Above all, keep fervent in your love for one another, because love covers a multitude of sins. Be hospitable to one another without complaint. As each one has received a *special* gift, employ it in serving one another as good stewards of the manifold grace of God. (1 Pet. 4:8-10).

What covers the multitude of your sins? The blood of Christ. When we love, we extend Christ's love, and so help one another to walk in the newness of our life in Christ. We remind one another that there is no condemnation or wrath for us, we are secure in Christ's love. We will carry this out, much like Paul's instructions to the Galatians in chapter 6, by bearing one another's burdens. Burdens, sins. We bear one another to the cross, we look together. We pray, we find hope, we reassure our hearts of His love shown at the cross. We find sweet relief for our angst when we are reminded that our sins are covered, His love never changes, never fails. The love we have for one another also causes us to use the gifts given us by the Lord to serve one another. Have you ever sat down to ponder the 'manifold grace of God?' Manifold, numerous, various, diverse. Let that open your imagination as you ponder your place in the church, in true fellowship with other believers. You have purpose, beloved. Each one of us is called to serve in the church. Though most of us will serve in unofficial capacities, we are not all pastors and elders, but we are all important.

All of this can be done well when we heed the call to '... all of you, clothe yourselves with humility toward one another' (1 Pet. 5:5b). Paul had the same idea in mind as he reminded the Galatians:

> For all of you who were baptized into Christ have clothed yourselves with Christ. There is neither Jew nor Greek, there is neither slave nor free man, there is neither male nor female; for you are all one in Christ Jesus (Gal. 3:27-28).

Everyone's worth in Christ is determined solely on being united to Christ; there is no value distinction. No DNA, no societal class, no sex, no quality we can think of will impress God or make Him shrink back. God's love draws us all into Christ and keeps us there, uniting us in peace and giving us a chance to finally enjoy one another rather than judge or mistreat one another.

Much like we are renewed (remember chapter seven?) for life in Christ, we are renewed for life within His body. Though Paul said he thanked God for having seen their love for all the saints, he still instructed the Colossians in how to further that love (see Col. 1:3-5 before moving on).

So, as those who have been chosen of God, holy and beloved, put on a heart of compassion, kindness, humility, gentleness and patience; bearing with one another, and forgiving each other, whoever has a complaint against anyone; just as the Lord forgave you, so also should you. Beyond all these things *put on* love, which is the perfect bond of unity. Let the peace of Christ rule in your hearts, to which indeed you were called in one body; and be thankful. Let the word of Christ richly dwell within you, with all wisdom teaching and admonishing one another ... (Col. 3:12-16).

This passage is not to be taken lightly but it would be a good one to read daily as you ask the Lord to teach you to love His body. These directives make little sense if we have not already pondered Christ's forgiveness, His peace (perhaps see John 14:25-29), and sought out His Word that it may dwell within you.

There are times when we are tempted to choose friendship according to the world; we make alliances and stick to them rather than clinging to Christ together. If we love one another as He did, we do not choose to stray with a friend, we call them back in love. In all our encouraging of one another, admonishing of one another, teaching of one another, and otherwise partaking in true fellowship with one another, we do not call one another to our own agenda, to our varied opinions, to our idealistic picture of fellowship. In several Epistles believers are expected to reprove and admonish one another (Romans, Ephesians, Colossians, 1 and 2 Thessalonians). We cannot walk in His light if we pretend our friends never need admonishing. We cannot walk in love if we overlook the sins of others, or if we react in anger to the loving admonishment directed at our sins. And so as we relate to one another, and come to find out that a brother or sister is not clinging to Christ, but is deceived and sinning, we love, we pray, we reprove. We shine the light of Christ, and that light is goodness, righteousness, truth (see Eph. 4). We often try to go about life without sharing divine truth, why is that?

Jesus taught that to love Him is to keep His commands, and they cannot be kept but by believing and obeying. And in this way we receive the blessing of joy. We need to cultivate a desire for that joy for one another. Then we will not allow others to stray without attempting to turn them back. Jesus spoke much that was intended for our joy (see John 17:13-14). In His presence is fullness of joy and the fellowship with the brethren ought to be a sharing of that joy.

Practices

Spend a couple months in the New Testament, making a list of 'one another' passages. As you journal these, pray for fellowship with people who will engage in this with you. Before you begin, turn to Leviticus 19:9-18. Our motivation for seeking and living in this love ought to be that our God has revealed this as His desire, He says: 'I am the LORD.' When our motivation for seeking fellowship is finding people who can 'meet my needs,' you will soon tarnish the fellowship. You will soon find yourself leaving to find another church to meet your needs. Start in the Gospel of John chapter 13 and work forward through Jude. You will find some verses do not have the words 'one another' but they do contain a directive for community life, such as 1 Corinthians 10:24 which tells us to seek the good of those in our community rather than our own good.

14

Retreat

This will be the most 'how to' of all the chapters in this book and I pray it will be a refreshing challenge as you near the end. In a world of distractions, it is the little habits that will make or break us. It is how we use the little moments that adds up. Either towards a life walking in the Spirit and filled with His life and peace. Or towards a life that feels hurried, urgent yet unimportant, like a hamster on his wheel. Or maybe even a hamster on his wheel with danger creeping up behind you (Agh! Run faster! Wait, where am I going?!).

Sometimes, to break a cycle, or simply to follow Jesus' custom, we come away. We rest for a period of time other than the Sabbath. It may be a few hours on a random morning, an entire day, a weekend, a week. In a world of distractions it will prove most necessary; in a world of selfish dreams it is a refreshing way to recalibrate. In a world full of idols competing for your affection, it is good to get away with your first love. As Paul told Timothy to ' ... kindle afresh the gift of God that is in you ...' and to 'Guard, through the Holy Spirit who dwells in us, the treasure which has been entrusted to *you*' (2 Tim. 1:6, 14) so we too need time to kindle afresh the gift of life, the gift of faith (read through Ephesians 1–2 looking for all that is included in this 'gift of God,' and note this is not an exhaustive list). Look for the treasure He has entrusted to us all (perhaps a time away asking the Lord to teach you what this treasure is).

As was Jesus' custom, make this custom yours too. Jesus went away often to pray and He found special places to go be alone for this purpose (gardens, mountaintops). He told His disciples to 'Come away by yourselves to a secluded place and rest for a while' (see Mark 6:31) even while there were pressing needs all about them. Sometimes we too need to partake in some means of grace that it feels otherwise difficult to fit into our schedules. The old adage of being too heavenly minded to be of any earthly good is the type of wisdom James denounces as earthly, sensual, demonic. The wisdom from above reminds us to look to Him when we are weary, trust Him to hold the universe together even though we are not working, trust Him to meet pressing needs even though we retreat. And history shows that those whose hope in Christ is strong are the most active in manifesting His truth and love and light in their communities.

I think it worth noting that Scripture does not allow us to desire or embark upon the life of a monk. We are not to run away from the world, or from fellowship, or from taking an active part in a local body of believers. The Lord has called us each to a life within the community and sphere where He has placed us. Most of us are called to lead a quiet life, loving our neighbors, loving our families, doing many of the same things each day. Preparing food, washing laundry, running errands, time on the clock, attending meetings, going to the office, mail, email, more errands, repairing vehicles, upkeep of a home and yard, caring for aging parents, and cleaning up all kinds of messes. Hobbies? Oh hopefully. The life we lead need not be filled with only urgent tasks. But it sometimes feels as if this is the only way. Let this weary feeling propel you to seek comfort, strength, wisdom, and times of refreshing that the Lord gives when you come away for a bit.

This will look different in various seasons of life. As a young professional I was able to reserve at least two vacation days each year to get away by myself. I would head to a local park or nearby National Park, sit in the midst of His creation, and enjoy a time without distractions. In addition, each vacation with my husband afforded many moments to 'retreat' as it were. As a young mom, it was an hour away in between breastfeeding. As a mom of young school age children, it was a weekend away.

For a day away, pick a location that you can be in all day. Not a coffee shop, the idea is to leave the world of distractions, and staying all day is not good for most budgets (how many pastries do you plan to consume anyway?). Although some may abhor the outdoors, it is the ideal location for being still and knowing He is God. Plan ahead so it is a time of year you'll want to be outdoors. I recommend a nearby State or National Park. I packed my lunch, a thermos of coffee, Bible, journal, hymnal, camera. There is no cell phone reception in the park I frequent which is all the better for leaving distractions behind. Though not to worry, there is a lodge nearby, and I was within walking distance of a bathhouse. I would sit near a stream at the foot of a mountain. I would dangle my feet off a bridge. I sang. I prayed. I journaled. I read, and read some more. I pondered and prayed through the passages. By the end of the afternoon my mind, heart, and body felt rested and refreshed. How wonderful are the effects of such times on our brains, hormones, and overall wellbeing. The whole human person (mind, body, heart) is interwoven, each part impacting the others and being out in creation, with time away from typical duties, refreshes the whole person.

I suggest picking a passage to focus on beforehand, a simple plan of where to start, knowing that He will meet you and teach you, and give you what you need in this time. Sometimes, what I need most is to spend time rehearsing things God has taught me recently, by reading through past journals. And then, running through my personal mission statement, reminding myself of God's work in me, the beauty of where He has put me, the goodness of His plans for little old me. The world values what earns the most money. God values His glory. We glorify Him most when our hearts delight in doing all things unto Him. He is not glorified by our chasing after dream homes, dream cars, dream jobs, dream abilities and vacations, and 'me time.' This extended time away may just reveal some of the idols you've been asking Him to bless, and the ways you've been avoiding His glory.

This personal retreat may be just the time to ask yourself whether you are seeking first God's kingdom, His beauty, His goodness, His truth. Or whether you have been asking Him to bless your hamster wheel. When you abide in His Word, it will direct your desires and prayers. And in line with His will, God will fill you as Paul prayed for the Ephesians:

> That He would grant you, according to the riches of His glory, to be strengthened with power through His Spirit in the inner man, so that Christ may dwell in your hearts through faith; *and* that you, being rooted and grounded in love, may be able to comprehend with all the saints what is the breadth and length and height and depth, and to know the love of Christ which surpasses knowledge, that you may be filled up to all the fullness of God.
>
> Now to Him who is able to do far more abundantly beyond all that we ask or think, according to the power that works within

us, to Him *be* the glory in the church and in Christ Jesus to all generations forever and ever. Amen (Eph. 3:16-21).

Ephesians is a personal favorite for times of refreshing, for realigning my desires, for being reminded of God's glory and love.

If planning a personal retreat sounds intimidating, start small. I have often taken any cancelled meetings as an opportunity to go to a nearby park, or to a grassy place with a mountain view near the office. Bible, journal, water, snack, coffee, blanket. And the otherwise wasted hour became an impromptu retreat. This time will grow so sweet that you will know an afternoon away is but a drop in the bucket.

When I was a young mom, adjusting to life with a new baby, I took every moment of undistracted time as a gift to focus, to set my mind. It is easy to waste these moments thinking I deserve a break. Time is a gift to steward well, not my personal property to waste. So an hour away at a coffee shop, in a corner booth, Bible and journal, coffee and pastry. And indeed the time was over too soon. But the Lord meets our needs in every season, and it is not good to fret over the past season of entire days being spent in the mountains. Being thankful in all things led me to see the joy of retreating for a moment, and the joy of being mindful in all the little moments in between (praying while nursing, memorizing Romans 5 while rocking a sleeping baby, listening to audio Bible while marching around the room trying to get a crying baby to relax).

As a mom of school age children, they have no needs that I alone must fill. Husbands and wives ought to coordinate so that each gets time away as a personal retreat with the Lord. I chose to return to the mountains, staying in a lodge in the midst of sheer beauty. The sights, sounds and smells of His creation did wonders for my weary soul. Elongated times in the Word, with no interruptions, journaling and pondering, and enjoying good meals. An afternoon near a cool mountain stream, a hike after dinner, taking in the morning from my balcony, hot coffee in hand. I read through Ezekiel, a book I hadn't focused on in a couple years and found great refreshment. I read through portions of the *Westminster Confession*. I journaled through prayers and passages, as the Lord dealt with my heart struggles in His mercy and compassion. This time away may never seem convenient, but it will be fruitful. Away from the usual, giving yourself time to lean into Him, to listen, to pray, to study and contemplate. You will be refreshed to return, to walk in the daily things He calls you to.

Once you have your Scripture picked out wherein you will focus your reading and prayer time, perhaps you would also like to pick a topic. Find the corresponding Scripture passages, and go with that in mind. For example, the prayers found in the Epistles, or the teaching found in Romans and Hebrews and Peter concerning perseverance and endurance. Open your time in a Psalm that draws your heart to worship and honor the Lord. This is, after all, more about being with God than about being away from others.

Give yourself time to sit and think setting your mind on the Spirit; look around and praise God for His works. Listen to the sounds He has created and feel your blood pressure lower. Take deep breaths. Think through a favorite hymn, let the verses guide you in prayer.

As you drive home, pray for the relationships in your life. After all, God fills us up to be in relationship with Himself and others. Time alone ought to refresh our souls and ready us for abiding in His love, truth, and grace among others.

15

A Parting Word

I humbly submit that this is my desire. To abide in my redeemer, in His love and His truth, deeper every day. Being still, knowing the one true God, and delighting in Him. Resting in His embrace whether the day be full of difficulty or ease. Pressing on to take hold of the eternal life that Christ won for me. I want to fight the good fight of the faith, resisting every contrary word that would draw me away from the simplicity and purity of devotion to Christ. I am trusting God to work this in me, in my family, in my church, in my community, in His world. Trusting God alone to fill me, as the sap from the vine fills the branches and makes them fruitful. It is my desire that these meditations would spur you on to study and ponder the Word of God, and dig into good books of faithful teachers, whose boast is in Christ alone.

To this end, the letters to the Ephesians and Colossians should be read by us often. Ephesians 1–2 are a beautiful reminder of how God has been working out His redemptive plan since before creating the world. None of God's work has been an afterthought. So as He chose you and made you anew, and lavished His grace upon you, and is now still building up His kingdom, none of these works were an afterthought either. He created us for His glory, created us anew in Christ with good works set aside for us to walk in. He has sealed us with His Spirit, the Spirit of truth who is our anointing, and who faithfully teaches us (see Ephesians 1:13; and 1 John 2). He has spoken to us in His Son, has guarded all that was written that we may abide in these precious words. These Epistles remind us to lift our gaze heavenward when the world would bog us down. Look to Christ rather than grow weary, for He is our life, He will minister to our every need. We need time to soak in the joy and wonder of His choosing us, all to His glory, and according to His kindness and good pleasure.

Meditate on our inheritance to free our affections from the passing things this world offers. As we lift our gaze and meditate on these things, God's words and His love will shape our thoughts, emotions, reactions, and our prayer life. Then we are more deeply abiding and will not be unfruitful. Dare we look for more, for what some would call a 'more personal' word? Is His Word not personal enough, the Word of His cross? And His resurrection? No beloved, do not be led astray from the deep simplicity to which you were called. Beware of false teachers who would add to God's Word, or who would tell you to look for something more. We read, we cling, we remember, we call to mind, and accept the Word implanted. We preach His words to our soul and share them with one another. We pray. And we await our homecoming.

Christian Focus Publications

Our mission statement —

STAYING FAITHFUL

In dependence upon God we seek to impact the world through literature faithful to His infallible Word, the Bible. Our aim is to ensure that the Lord Jesus Christ is presented as the only hope to obtain forgiveness of sin, live a useful life and look forward to heaven with Him.

Our books are published in four imprints:

CHRISTIAN
FOCUS

Popular works including biographies, commentaries, basic doctrine and Christian living.

CHRISTIAN
HERITAGE

Books representing some of the best material from the rich heritage of the church.

MENTOR

Books written at a level suitable for Bible College and seminary students, pastors, and other serious readers. The imprint includes commentaries, doctrinal studies, examination of current issues and church history.

CF4•K

Children's books for quality Bible teaching and for all age groups: Sunday school curriculum, puzzle and activity books; personal and family devotional titles, biographies and inspirational stories — because you are never too young to know Jesus!

Christian Focus Publications Ltd,
Geanies House, Fearn, Ross-shire,
IV20 1TW, Scotland, United Kingdom.
www.christianfocus.com
blog.christianfocus.com